A–Z
OF
HOUSEHOLD
HINTS

A – Z
OF
HOUSEHOLD
HINTS

by

Christine Green

PAPERFRONTS

Typeset in 10/10½pt Times by County Typesetters, Margate, Kent.

Printed and Bound in Great Britain by Clays Ltd., Bungay, Suffolk.

The *Paperfronts* series and the *Right Way* series are both published by Elliot Right Way Books, Brighton Road, Lower Kingswood, Tadworth, Surrey, KT20 6TD, U.K.

CONTENTS

To my family and mother
– for all their support

1

STAIN REMOVAL HINTS

Introduction
Every household should have a store of stain removers in the cupboard. A suggested list is given below.

Check that: each substance is well labelled; securely stored safely away from children/animals; when using some of the more toxic ones that a window is left open; instructions are closely followed.

Biological Detergent
Deep seated stains react well to a soak in diluted biological detergent.

Bleach
Always dilute according to instructions and rinse article well afterwards.

Borax
Available from chemists, it is generally made up to a paste by adding water.

Methylated Spirit
Generally used neat. Highly flammable, so store safely.

Turpentine/White Spirit
Generally used neat. Highly flammable, so store safely.

Household Ammonia
Generally diluted – handle with care and wear rubber gloves. This is poisonous, so store safely.

Grease Solvents
These come in a variety of forms; ie. liquid, paste, spray, etc. It is important that you check the manufacturer's instructions to see whether the product is applicable to the particular stain you are treating.

White Vinegar
Ideal for removing paint stains.

Glycerine
Useful for removing paint stains.

Salt
Makes a good absorbing agent.

Washing Soda
Ideal for removing greasy stains. Wear rubber gloves as it tends to burn.

General Tips
1 *Always* check the washing instructions on the garment before using *any* stain removal tip from this book.
2 Stains are easier to remove when they have just happened, so act quickly. Never rub a stain as this may harm the fabric and spread the mark.
3 Use a piece of white cloth (an old sheet is ideal). Coloured cloth could bleed dye and make the stain worse.
4 Work inwards, thereby not spreading the stain.
5 Don't let carpets get too wet.
6 Those with sensitive skins should wear rubber gloves when using any of the substances.

Definition of Terms

Washable fabrics include: acetate; acrylic; denim; cotton; cheesecloth; gingham; net; linen; polyester; towelling; winceyette; lace; nylon; serge; viyella.

Non-washable fabrics include: brocade; felt; leather; suede; gabardine; hessian; moire; cotton; silk; metallic yarns.

Acid

The kinds of products which leave acid stains include: vinegar; fruit juice; lemon juice; beetroot.

Washable: Rub the area with a damp sponge. To counteract the acid combine 1 tablespoon of borax with 1 pt (560ml) warm water; work this well into the stain. Rinse with clean water and blot dry with tissues (wear gloves when using borax if you have sensitive skin).

Non-washable: Dab with cold water until the stain has gone.

Carpets: Rub the area with a damp sponge.

Adhesives

There are various kinds of adhesives, here are some of the common ones.

ANIMAL/FISH GLUE BASED:
Washable: Wash as usual.

Non-washable: Take to dry cleaners.

Carpets: See washable.

CONTACT ADHESIVE:
Washable: Wash the garment in cold water immediately. If the glue has hardened then use methylated spirit.

Non-washable: Take to dry cleaners.

Carpets: Rub the area with a damp sponge. If stain persists try methylated spirit, rub with clean water and blot dry.

EPOXY:
Washable: Apply methylated spirit quickly, before glue hardens.

Non-washable: Take to dry cleaners.

Carpets: See washable.

LATEX:
Washable: Wipe with a wet cloth. If dry, remove with a flat-bladed knife.

Non-washable: Take to dry cleaners.

Carpets: See washable.

SUPERGLUE:
Washable: Act quickly, hold under running cold water, carefully prise apart.

Non-washable: Take to dry cleaners.

Carpets: Quickly rub the area with a damp sponge. Then peel off the glue.

Ballpoint Ink
Washable: Rub methylated spirit over the area with a cloth. Wash in cold water. Finally wash as usual.

Non-washable: Take to dry cleaners.

Carpets: Rub some methylated spirit onto the carpet. Dab with a damp cloth, then blot dry using tissues.

Beer
Washable: Steep in biological detergent; wash as usual.
Stubborn stains – combine 1 part white vinegar to 5 parts warm water, and sponge over the material. Rinse, then wash as usual.

Non-washable: Make up the vinegar mixture as above, and apply this to the area with a sponge. Rinse with cold water.

Carpets: Wipe over with a cloth soaked in warm water.
Stubborn stains – try the vinegar solution, rinse and rub the area with a damp sponge.

Beetroot
Washable: Dab lots of cold water over the garment. Rub washing-up liquid into the stain. Steep overnight in biological detergent – wash as usual.
Stubborn stain – put some borax over the stain, then pour boiling water through. Rinse, then wash as usual.

Non-washable: Dab cold water over the area, then take to dry cleaners.

Carpets: Dab with cold water, then absorb the water with a wad of towelling. Use a carpet shampoo.

Bird Droppings
Washable: Remove the droppings; wipe over with tepid salted water. Steep overnight in biological detergent. Wash as usual.

Non-washable: Combine 6 parts warm water with 1 part ammonia and sponge it over the area (make sure you wear rubber gloves to protect your hands). Using a sponge rinse with warm water, then spot the area with white wine vinegar. Dab with a wet sponge then blot dry.

Blood
Washable: Steep garment in a strong salt and cold water solution for an hour (hot water seals the protein in blood). Keep changing the water until it runs clear. Steep in biological detergent and cold water. Wash again in cold water.
Stubborn stains – combine 2 teaspoons ammonia with 1 pt (560ml) cold water plus a few drops of hydrogen peroxide (make sure you wear gloves to protect your hands). Test on an inside piece to ensure colour isn't affected. Soak the garment in this. Rinse and wash as usual.

Non-washable: Rub the stains with cold water and then take to dry cleaners.

Carpets: Rub stains with cold water and towel dry. Follow up with a carpet shampoo if necessary.

Butter
Washable: Scrape away as much as possible. Rub washing-up liquid into the stain, wash in a biological detergent.

Non-washable: Scrape away as much of the butter as possible. Rub the stain with a small amount of washing-up liquid then sponge off with warm water. A dry cleaner may be required for larger stains.

Carpets: Use a carpet shampoo.

Candle Spills
Washable: If soft, put it into the freezer until it hardens. Sandwich the marked area between blotting paper then press with a warm iron. Keep changing the paper around so that clean areas cover the spot; the warmth from the iron should melt the wax, and the blotting paper soak it up.

Non-washable: As for washable, take to the dry cleaners after ironing.

Carpets: If soft, pack ice cubes around the area until the grease has solidified, then pick off. Place blotting paper on the carpet and press as for washable. If a mark remains, use a carpet shampoo.

Charcoal
Washable: Wash immediately in biological detergent and warm water.

Non-washable: Sponge area with warm water – take to dry cleaners.

Carpets: Sponge over with warm water then follow up with a carpet shampoo.

Chewing Gum
Washable: Put the item into the fridge until the gum has hardened, then pick it off. Wash as normal.

Non-washable: As above, but instead of washing, take to the dry cleaners.

Carpets: Pack ice cubes around the area, then apply some white spirit on a clean cloth. If a mark remains, use a carpet shampoo.

Chocolate
Washable: Rub with washing-up liquid, then steep in warm water and biological detergent.
Stubborn stain – make a solution of 1 tablespoon of borax, 1 pt (560ml) warm water and sponge this over the stain. Rinse and wash.

Non-washable: Take to dry cleaners.

Carpets: Use a carpet shampoo.

Cigarette Burns – see also *Scorch Marks,* page 27.
Washable: Rub washing-up liquid into the scorch mark.

Dab with a solution of 1 tablespoon of borax and 1 pt (560ml) warm water, then wash as usual.

Non-washable: Take to dry cleaners.

Carpets: Rub the burnt fibres with fine sandpaper then make up the solution as above and dab on the carpet. Follow this by dabbing warm water over the area, then absorb any surplus liquid with a towel.

Coffee
Washable: Steep overnight in warm water and a biological detergent.
Stubborn stains – make a solution of 1 tablespoon of borax, 1 pt (560ml) warm water and sponge over stain. Rinse and wash.

Non-washable: Dab area with a borax solution as above, then dab clean with fresh water.

Carpets: Spraying with a soda syphon works wonders! Otherwise dab clean with warm water and a biological detergent.

Crayons
Washable: Rub washing-up liquid into the stain.
Stubborn stains – rub with methylated spirit on a clean cloth, wash off with cold water. Wash as usual.

Non-washable: Take to dry cleaners.

Carpets: See washable.

Cream
Washable: Remove surplus. Wash in cold water. Steep in biological detergent.
Stubborn stain – may need to use a dry cleaning solvent.

Non-washable: Try using a dry cleaning solvent, failing

that take to dry cleaners.

Carpets: Try using a dry cleaning solvent, then use a carpet shampoo.

Curry
Washable: Wash in warm water to remove most of the stain. Rub with glycerine to loosen the stain, then rinse the article in warm water. Wash as usual.

Non-washable: Dab area with a solution of 1 tablespoon of borax and 1 pt (560ml) warm water, leave to soak for 15 minutes and then rinse.

Carpets: As for non-washable.

Drip Marks
To dispel drip marks under taps, rub the marks with warm vinegar then rinse with hot water. Do this daily until the mark disappears.

Dye
Washable: Rinse immediately in cold water. Steep over-night in cold water and a biological detergent.
Stubborn stains – make up a solution 1 part hydrogen peroxide, 6 parts water. Making sure you wear rubber gloves to protect your hands, sponge the stain then rinse with cold water.

Non-washable: Take to dry cleaners.

Carpets: Dab area with cold water and absorb any surplus. For small splashes, use methylated spirit.

Egg
Washable: Wash out in cold water. Steep overnight in warm water and biological detergent.

Non-washable: Gently rub with washing-up liquid and

cold water. May require a grease solvent which can be bought in spray, paste or aerosol form. They may be purchased under various trade names but instructions must be carefully followed.

Carpets: As non-washable.
Stubborn stain – use a carpet shampoo.

Engine Oil
Washable: Apply neat liquid detergent or oil of eucalyptus onto the stain then wash in biological detergent. Another alternative is to use petrol in a similar manner but beware: it is highly inflammable so use with care. Rinse and dry.
Stubborn stain – try a dry cleaning solvent.

Non-washable: Take to dry cleaners.

Carpets: Blot up excess. Put some white spirit on cotton wool and rub this into the stain. Follow with a carpet shampoo.

Faeces
Washable: Scrape off the excess. If the stain isn't too bad wash it in some biological detergent then rinse thoroughly.

Non-washable: Scrape off the surplus. Take to the dry cleaners.

Carpets: Scrape off the surplus then dab with sponge soaked in water. If the stain is solid use a pet stain remover to soften it. Disinfect the area and, if necessary, follow with a carpet shampoo.

Felt Tipped Pens
Washable: Rub glycerine over, then wash.
Stubborn stain – dab the area with methylated spirit. Rinse off with cold water then wash.

Non-washable: Dab with methylated spirit for small stains.
Larger stains should be taken to the dry cleaners.

Carpets: Use a carpet shampoo.

Fruit Stains
Washable: Hold under a cold water tap until water runs clean. Steep in biological detergent and warm water.
Stubborn stain – solution of 1 part hydrogen peroxide, 6 parts water (make sure you wear gloves). Do a test patch first to check for any signs of the colour running, but if it doesn't, steep in the solution. Rinse and wash.

Non-washable: Dab area with warm water and take to the dry cleaners.

Carpets: Absorb any surplus liquid with a cloth and treat with a carpet shampoo.

Glue – see *Adhesives*

Grass
Washable: Light stains – ordinary washing should suffice.
Stubborn stains – rub methylated spirit into the mark, rinse and wash in the usual way.

Non-washable: Make up an even quantity of cream of tartar, salt and water. Put onto the stain and leave to dry. Brush out.
Stubborn stains – take to dry cleaner.

Gravy
Washable: Slight stain – immerse in cold water, and then wash in biological detergent.
Stubborn stain – generally gravy has a grease base and it may therefore be necessary to use a grease solvent before washing a garment with a stubborn stain in hot water and biological detergent.

Non-washable: Do a test patch with a grease solvent. If the colours bleed, take to dry cleaners.

Carpets: Rub in dry cleaning fluid then follow up with a carpet shampoo.

Grease
Washable: Remove the surplus grease then sprinkle some talcum powder over. Brush away the powder then use a suitable dry cleaning solvent to remove any remaining grease stain. Wash the garment in very hot water.

Non-washable: Remove the surplus grease then sprinkle talcum powder over. Brush away the powder then use a suitable dry cleaning solvent. If stain remains take the garment to the dry cleaners.

Carpets: Absorb any surplus grease with kitchen towelling then sprinkle some talcum powder over. Vacuum, and if the stain remains treat with a carpet shampoo.

Hair Dye
Washable: Steep in cold water then rub washing-up liquid into stain. Immerse in biological detergent and warm water. Keep changing the water until it is clean. Wash as usual.

Non-washable: Rub washing-up liquid into the stain and sponge it off using warm water. If the stain remains, take the garment to the dry cleaners.

Carpets: Dab with cold water, then rub washing-up liquid into stain, working from the outside of the stain to the middle.
Stubborn stain – use carpet shampoo.

Hairspray
Washable: Rub washing-up liquid into the back of the stain. Rinse and wash.

Non-washable: Take to dry cleaners.

Carpets: Sponge over with white spirit then use a carpet shampoo.

Honey (and Jam)
Washable: Steep in warm water and biological detergent. Rub thoroughly, rinse, then dry.
Stubborn stains – steep in 1 tablespoon borax and 1 pt (560ml) warm water, rinse and wash.

Non-washable: Remove any surplus honey with a cloth. You may then be able to rinse in cold water and rub in washing-up liquid. (Generally non-washable fabrics withstand being rinsed in cold water, just so long as it is not done too often. However, always check the garment label.)

Carpets: Remove any surplus honey with a cloth, dab with warm water, then use a carpet shampoo.

Ice Cream
Washable: Remove any surplus ice cream with a cloth. Steep in biological detergent and warm water, wash.
Stubborn stain – make up a solution of 1 tablespoon borax with 1 pt (560ml) of warm water, and rub in to the area. Rinse.

Non-washable: Dab with biological detergent and warm water.
Stubborn stain – take to dry cleaners.

Carpets: Rub washing-up liquid into the stain – remove with a little warm water.
Stubborn stain – use a carpet shampoo.

Ink – see also *Ballpoint Ink,* page 10.
Washable: Hold under cold water tap and rub liquid detergent into the back of the stain whilst still under

water.
Stubborn stain – rub a mixture of lemon juice and salt.
Rinse and then wash as usual.

Non-washable: Take to dry cleaners.

Carpets: Give a squirt from a soda syphon then absorb any
surplus liquid with a cloth. If you don't have a soda
syphon then you can use a plant waterer or for small spots
use an eye drop applicator. Do this several times, then use
a carpet shampoo.

Iron Mould

This is caused when a garment has had something which is
rusting placed on it.
Washable: Rub lemon juice and salt into light stains and
let stand for 1 hour before rinsing thoroughly. Repeat if
necessary.

Non-washable: Dry cleaners.

Carpets: The salt and lemon juice mixture might work,
otherwise call professional help.

Jam – see *Honey,* page 19.

Ketchup

Washable: Remove any surplus ketchup with a cloth.
Steep in cold water, then rub washing-up liquid into the
stain, wash as usual
Stubborn stain – steep in 6 parts water, 1 part hydrogen
peroxide (make sure you wear rubber gloves).

Non-washable: Rub washing-up liquid into stain. Clean
off with warm water.
Larger stains – take to dry cleaners.

Carpets: Loosen the mark by rubbing in glycerine and
warm water. Clean off with warm water and a biological

detergent. Rinse and absorb any surplus with a cloth.

Lipstick
Washable: Rub petroleum jelly or glycerine into the stain, clean off with warm water. Wash as usual.

Non-washable: Remove any surplus with a cloth – then take to the dry cleaners.

Carpets: Rub washing-up liquid into the stain and sponge with warm water.
Stubborn stain – use a carpet shampoo.

Make-up
Washable: Remove any surplus with a cloth, sprinkle talcum powder over the stain to absorb grease. Rub washing-up liquid into the stain, clean off with cold water, wash as usual.
Stubborn stain – soak in a solution 1 teaspoon ammonia, 1 pt (560ml) water (make sure you wear rubber gloves). Rinse and wash.

Non-washable: Small marks – dab with methylated spirit. Larger stains – take to dry cleaners.

Carpets: Rub washing-up liquid into stain and sponge with warm water. Then use a carpet shampoo.

Mayonnaise
Washable: Remove any surplus with a cloth. Rub washing-up liquid into stain. Steep overnight in biological detergent and warm water.
Stubborn stain – use a grease solvent, rinse and wash.

Non-washable: Rub washing-up liquid into a small stain. Sponge off with warm water.
Larger stains – take to dry cleaners.

Carpets: Try washing-up liquid then sponge off and use a

carpet shampoo.

Medicine
Washable: Steep in cold water. Wash.
Stubborn stain – rub methylated spirit into stain. Rinse and wash.

Non-washable: Take to dry cleaners.

Carpets: Squirt with a soda syphon, or clean with several applications of cold water. Absorb the liquid with a cloth after each squirt/application. It may be necessary to use a carpet shampoo.

Metal Polish
Washable: Absorb any surplus with a cloth. Rub in white spirit on a clean cloth. Rinse and wash.

Non-washable: Rub washing-up liquid into the stain. Sponge-rinse with a touch of warm water.

Carpets: Rub in white spirit on a clean cloth. Use a carpet shampoo for any remaining stains.

Mildew
This is caused when clothes are put away damp.
Washable: Ordinary laundering should remove stain.
For stubborn stains on white cotton or linen, steep it in a solution of 1 tablespoon bleach with 2 pts (1.1 litres) water.
Steep other fabrics in a solution 1 part hydrogen peroxide, 6 parts water, making sure you wear rubber gloves.

Non-washable: Take to dry cleaners.

Carpets: Dab area with some antiseptic diluted in warm water. Wipe clean and absorb any excess with a cloth.

Milk
Washable: Steep in cold running water. Wash.
Stubborn stain – steep in a solution 1 tablespoon borax,
1 pt (560ml) warm water. Rinse and wash.

Non-washable: Apply area with solution as above. Clean
with warm water then absorb surplus with a cloth.

Carpets: Squirt soda syphon over or several applications
of warm water. Absorb surplus with a cloth. Finish off
with carpet shampoo.

Mud
Washable: Attempting to remove mud when it is still wet
only causes it to go deeper into the fabric. It is better to
wait until it has dried. When the mud is dry, scrape off the
surplus then steep in biological detergent and warm water.
Then wash.

Non-washable: Leave until the mud has dried. Remove
the surplus with a stiff brush. Rub neat washing-up liquid
into the stain. Clean with warm water and absorb
moisture with a cloth.

Carpets: Vacuum the dried mud. Treat any remaining
stain with carpet shampoo.

Mustard
Washable: Steep in biological detergent and warm water.
Wash.
Stubborn stain – steep in solution 1 tablespoon ammonia,
1 pt (560ml) warm water (make sure you wear rubber
gloves). Rinse well.

Non-washable: Clean with cold water.
Stubborn stain – take to dry cleaners.

Carpets: Squirt soda syphon or several applications of
clean water. Absorb surplus with a cloth. Finish by

treating with carpet shampoo if necessary.

Nail Varnish
Washable: Absorb any surplus with a cloth, then apply white spirit on the back of the stain. Rinse and wash as usual. If the stain has dried, soften it by rubbing some glycerine in.

Non-washable: Take to dry cleaners.

Carpets: Absorb surplus, dabbing with cloth soaked with white spirit. Finish up using a carpet shampoo.

Newsprint
Washable: Apply some methylated spirit. Wash as usual.

Non-washable: Small marks can be dealt with by applying some methylated spirit.
Larger marks – take to dry cleaners.

Carpets: As for non-washable.

Paint
ACRYLIC:
Washable: Act speedily, rub washing-up liquid into stain. Soak in biological detergent and warm water.
Stubborn stain – use methylated spirit on clean cloth. Check material.

Non-washable: Put petroleum jelly over the area to keep moist then take to dry cleaners.

Carpets: Must be dealt with damp. Scrape off excess before tackling the stain with some methylated spirit. Follow up with a carpet shampoo.

CELLULOSE PAINT:
Washable: Sponge the back of the stain with cellulose thinner, then wash.

Non-washable: Take to dry cleaners.

Carpets: Treat the area with cellulose thinners. Follow up with a carpet shampoo.

EMULSION:
Washable: Hold under running cold tap and rub stain with fingers to release paint. Follow with a cool wash.

Non-washable: Apply petroleum jelly to the area, keeping it moist, then take to the dry cleaners.

Carpets: Plenty of cold water, then carpet shampoo if necessary.

GLOSS PAINT:
Washable: Rub area with turpentine or white spirit. Hold under cold running water, then wash. Before you do this, however, check that it is safe to use turpentine or white spirit on that item.

Non-washable: Take to dry cleaners.

Carpets: Rub the carpet with turpentine or white spirit. Follow with carpet shampoo.

OIL PAINT:
Washable: Treat with white spirit then rub washing-up liquid into stain. Rinse and wash.

Non-washable: Take to dry cleaners.

Carpets: Rub some white spirit onto the area, then massage neat washing-up liquid into the stain. Rub, then blot dry.

WATER COLOUR:
Washable: Steep in cold water and rub stain with fingers to release paint. Wash as normal.

Non-washable: Dab at small stains with cold water.
Larger area – take to dry cleaners.

Carpets: Sponge with cold water and a little ammonia
(make sure you wear rubber gloves).

Perfume
Washable: Soak in warm water and then wash.
Stubborn stain – rub in glycerine diluted in warm water.
Wash.

Non-washable: Sponge with cold water then take to dry
cleaners.

Carpets: Rub in glycerine diluted in warm water, then use
a carpet shampoo.

Perspiration
Washable: Steep in a biological detergent.
Stubborn stain – dab some neat ammonia over the stain,
then rinse (remember to wear gloves). Add 1 tablespoon
white distilled vinegar to ½ pt (280ml) warm water and
sponge this over the area if colour has been affected.
Wash as usual.

Non-washable: Make up the white distilled vinegar and
warm water solution then sponge the affected area of the
fabric. If stain remains take to the dry cleaners.

Petroleum Jelly
Washable: Rub washing-up liquid into stain. Wash.

Non-washable: Take to dry cleaners.

Carpets: Rub washing-up liquid into stain. Wash off and
absorb surplus with a cloth. Finish with carpet shampoo if
necessary.

Plasticine
Washable: Rub washing-up liquid into stain.
Stubborn stain – treat with a grease solvent, rinse, then wash.

Non-washable: Treat small areas with grease solvent.
Larger areas – take to dry cleaners.

Carpets: Use a carpet shampoo.

Rust
Washable: Lay the garment out in the sun and sprinkle some salt over the stained area. Put sufficient lemon juice over to dampen both the salt and fabric and leave it outdoors to dry in the sunshine. Rinse then wash.

Non-washable: Take to dry cleaners.

Carpets: Use a carpet shampoo.

Scorch Marks – see also *Cigarette Burns,* page 13.
Washable: A light mark can be removed by soaking the area in cold milk as soon as possible.
Other methods: soak cottons and linen in a mixture of 1 tablespoon bleach, 2 pts (1.1 litres) water (make sure you wear rubber gloves). Other fabrics can be treated by dabbing a solution of 1 tablespoon borax in 1 pt (560ml) warm water.

Non-washable: Sponge gently with a borax solution, rinse and blot dry.

Carpets: If marks have damaged the fibres, brush them over with fine sandpaper. Light marks can be treated by being lightly dampened, rubbed over with powdered borax, left to dry, then brushed off; sponge gently with a damp soapy cloth and then sponge with clean water.

Sea Water
Washable: Soak garment in warm water until it runs clear. Wash as normal.

Shoes: Dissolve ½ oz (12g) bicarbonate of soda in 4 tablespoons of hot milk and apply to the shoes with a sponge or cloth. Leave the solution to dry and then polish.

Shoe Polish
Washable: Deal with the stain by dabbing the area with some white spirit. Wash with biological detergent and hot water with a drop or two of ammonia added.

Non-washable: Use a paintbrush and dab the affected area with white spirit. A dry cleaning solvent works effectively too.

Carpets: As for non-washable. Finish with carpet shampoo.

Sock Stain
Add a teaspoon of bicarbonate of soda to the water in which you are washing to help restore them to their former whiteness.

Sun Tan Oil
Washable: Sponge fabric with a proprietary grease solvent laying a thick pad underneath.
Stubborn stains – soak garment in warm water with a tablespoon of borax. Then wash in biological detergent and rinse.

Non-washable: Dab with a grease solvent.

Carpets: Blot up excess. Put some white spirit on to cotton wool and rub it into the stain. Follow with a carpet shampoo.

Syrup
Washable: Act swiftly and soak the fabric in hot water and biological detergent whilst stain is moist. Rinse and dry. Stubborn stains – soak in 1 tablespoon borax and 1 pt (560ml) warm water, rinse and wash.

Non-washable: Remove any surplus syrup with a cloth. Sponge rinse in cold water then rub in washing-up liquid and rinse.

Carpets: Remove any surplus syrup with a cloth and some warm water. Then use a carpet shampoo.

Tar
Washable: Scrape away surplus, then soften any remaining tar with glycerine rubbed into it. Remove any remaining with eucalyptus oil, massaging it into the back of the garment. Wash in the hottest possible temperature it will stand.

Non-washable: Apply glycerine then dab with warm water.

Carpets: Scrape away surplus then soften with glycerine and use a grease solvent or eucalyptus oil.

Tea
Washable: Make up 1 tablespoon borax and 1 pt (560ml) water and rub over. Then steep in biological detergent and wash as usual.

Non-washable: Treat with a solution of 1 tablespoon borax to 1 pt (560ml) water then sponge and blot dry.

Carpets: As non-washable. If the tea contained milk, it may be necessary to use a carpet shampoo.

Urine
Washable: Steep in biological detergent and cold water, adding some disinfectant. Wash in very hot water.
Stubborn stains – mixture of 1 part hydrogen peroxide, 6 parts cold water (watch for colours running and keep hands protected).

Non-washable: Dab gently with biological detergent and warm water with disinfectant added. Dab rinse and dry.

Carpets: As for non-washable. If smell persists, follow with carpet shampoo.

Varnish
Washable: Dab with methylated spirit then wash in biological detergent and rinse.

Non-washable: Use methylated spirit.
Stubborn stain – take to dry cleaners.

Carpets: Treat as non-washable.

Wine
Washable: Red wine – sprinkle salt over the area, steep in cold water then rinse. Often white wine poured over red wine will extract some of the stain.
Stubborn stains – make up a solution of 1 tablespoon borax with 1 pt (560ml) warm water and steep the garment. Rinse and wash.
White wine – may be rinsed out.

Non-washable: Red wine – absorb with a cloth, then sprinkle talcum powder over the area.
Stubborn stains – take to dry cleaners.
White wine – as above.

Carpets: Red wine – try pouring white wine over the area, or a dash of soda. Pour talcum powder or salt over, and vacuum clean. Do this several times until the stain begins to fade.

Stubborn stains – dab methylated spirit over.
White wine – absorb surplus with a cloth, then apply some
tepid water with some detergent added.

2

DOMESTIC HINTS

Acrylic Garments
When washing, check that the water isn't too hot, no more than 40°C (104°F), otherwise permanent creases could occur which are difficult to remove.

Aluminium Foil
Aluminium foil has many uses: for wrapping up parcels; covering foods when cooking/storing; sculpturing models for youngsters; lining the grill pan when grilling foods; it's ideal for painting jobs, i.e. for lining the paint roller tin, and for covering brushes when having a break from painting so that the bristles keep pliable until your return.

Unless you have used aluminium foil for a particularly dirty job don't throw it away. Wash it in warm soapy water, give it a good rinse and when dry flatten it out for its next job!

Aluminium Pans
To remove bad stains from the bottom of pans, make up a solution 3 parts vinegar to 1 part water, and simmer it in the pan for 10 − 15 minutes. Bring a shine back to tarnished looking aluminium pans by boiling acidic fruits such as rhubarb or apples in them.

Angora – see also *Jumpers*, page 45; *Wool*, page 59.
This material requires a gentle wash and should be treated as you would sheep's wool.

Ants
To get rid of these unpleasant little creatures from your home, try to locate their nest or at least the places where they are gaining entry, and pour boiling water inside. Because ants don't like paraffin another effective method to get rid of them is to stuff the point of entry with cotton wool soaked in paraffin. There are also many effective insecticides available. For further information on dealing with pest control write to British Pest Control Association (see appendix).

Balloons
Ease the task of blowing up balloons by rolling and stretching them in your hands to loosen the plastic.

Bath – see also *Shower Curtain*, page 54.
For an inexpensive bubble bath and cleaner in one, add several capfuls of washing-up liquid to the running water. When finished, swill the water around the bath to get rid of any tidemarks. Don't do this, of course, if you're allergic to detergents.

Bath Mat
To keep a rubber mat soft, steep it in a bath full of warm water, occasionally topping it up to keep the temperature even. After an hour rub the mat dry.

Beakers
A thick elastic band or several spaced apart around a beaker will make it easier for the elderly and young to hold when using. See Fig. 1 (overleaf).

Fig. 1 Showing a beaker with several elastic bands spaced apart.

Beds, Airing – see also *Electric Overblankets,* page 39; *Electric Underblankets,* page 39; *Mattress Care,* page 47; *Pillow,* page 50; *Quilt Covers,* page 51.

To check whether a bed is aired, slip a small hand mirror in between the sheets for 10 minutes. If, when removed, it is even a little misty, the bed is not fully aired.

Belts

When making holes in leather or plastic belts use a hot metal knitting needle. Heat the knitting needle by holding the point over a lighter flame; it will only take a minute or two to warm up efficiently. When doing this make sure you wear an oven glove or similar protective glove!

Bicarbonate of Soda

Bicarbonate of soda has many uses: because it is an alkali it counteracts many mild acid stains and is useful if applied neat to a damp cloth in removing any marks on worktops or other general household equipment. Many people use bicarbonate for medicinal purposes; for example, for the relief of indigestion, and as a gargle for sore throats. It is used in the culinary world as a raising agent.

Blankets – see *Wool*, page 59.

Bottle Tops
There are several methods of opening a stiff bottle top; hold it under hot running water; wear a rubber glove to get a firmer grip; or pop it in the freezer for ten minutes.

Bread Bin
Soak a cloth in vinegar and rub it around the inside of a bread bin to stop mildew forming. Make sure the bin is left to dry out thoroughly before replacing any bread.

Cake Tins
To rustproof an old cake tin, wash and dry then smother it with lard and bake in a moderate oven for half an hour.

Candles
A candle too small to burn any longer has other uses: rubbed over ink-written addresses on parcels and garden labels, it will seal them and stop the ink from smearing in the rain. Also see *Drawers*, p. 38.

Carpet
Carpet which has flattened due to something heavy being placed on it can be revived by leaving an ice cube on the spot overnight. The following day hoover the carpet using the suction nozzle.

Carpet Underlay
A good underlay will extend the life of a carpet. If you can't afford underlay then at least use newspaper in a thickness of six sheets.

Caustic Soda

This strong cleaner is ideal for cleaning inside a dirty oven, to use as a paint stripper, and also for cleaning blocked drains (not those blocked by grease because it would make the grease solidify). Because it is highly poisonous, follow the instructions, keep it well away from children, and store safely. Always wear rubber gloves when handling.

Chair Covers

If chair covers are washed, and then replaced when still slightly damp, they can then be easily stretched into shape for a snug fitting.

Chamois Leather

Chamois leathers can be washed in warm soapy water. Then you can leave a lather of soap in the chamois, which keeps it soft, and let it dry without rinsing. Alternatively, rinse it, squeeze it but don't wring, then shake it out flat. Leave it to dry but away from direct heat. Once it is dry, then crumple it up to bring back the softness.

China – see *Ornaments,* page 49.

Cling Film

Prevent cling film from sticking to itself by storing it in the fridge.

Clothes, Shiny – see *Ironing,* page 44.

Cord, Decorative

A touch of clear nail varnish dabbed on either end of decorative cord will prevent it from fraying.

Crochet lengths of wool to make inexpensive wrapping cord.

Crayons

To harden wax crayons store them in the fridge

overnight.

Curtain Rails
Curtains will glide along the rail easier if the rail is sprayed with some furniture polish.

Cutlery
Silver cutlery will remain clean longer if wrapped in cling film after being polished.

Use water in which eggs have been boiled to remove the yellow egg yolk which has stuck on to the cutlery.

Decanter
To remove a discoloured stain from the bottom of a decanter break up some egg shell and put this, together with a little warm water, inside it. Give it a good shake and leave it to stand overnight. The following morning give it another good shake and wash it out in warm soapy water. Rinse thoroughly.

Diamond
To clean a diamond ring, soak it in an eggcup with a small amount of washing-up liquid and water, long enough to soften the dirt. Then clean with a toothbrush.

Dishes
To keep dishes warm if the oven is full, put them into the sink and cover with boiling water. Remove and dry as and when required.

Doors
Stop doors squeaking by spraying some washing-up liquid along the hinges. To prevent a door from sticking, run a candle along the closing edge.

Drains – see *Sink*, page 54.

Drawers
To prevent a drawer from sticking, run a candle along the runners.

Dresses
When pegging out a dress, hang it on a coat hanger and tie the hanger to the washing line firmly with a stocking.

Peg a pleated skirt up by the waistband; use plenty of pegs.

Dressing Table
If perfume bottles are stored inside the dressing table drawer, absorb any possible spills or leakages by lining the drawer with a sheet of blotting paper.

Dustbins
Wash out a plastic bin with a solution of bleach and water. Leave to dry in the fresh air for several hours.

Put some mothballs in the bottom of your dustbin to keep flies away.

Dusters – see *Washing*, page 57.

Duvet
Replace a clean duvet cover speedily by first turning it inside out. Slide your hands in and grab the first two corners, ease the cover over the end of the duvet. With the two corners firmly held, shake the cover and it will slide into place.

Dyeing Garments
Before dyeing any garment it is advisable to test on a hidden part of the fabric to make sure the resultant colour is that which you want. When dyeing a light coloured fabric black use equal quantities of blue and black dye to prevent that green tell-tale tinge which home dyed garments often have.

Electric Overblankets
These can be put on top of the bed and may be left on during the night.

Never switch on an electric blanket if there is any possibility it may be damp. An electric blanket should be professionally checked for safety at least every two years. Don't use when creased, the elements might have been damaged. When storing away, roll or lie the blanket flat. Never leave heavy objects on top of the electric blanket when switched on; this could cause the wires to overheat.

Electric Plug
To prevent a plug from sticking in its socket, rub each of the pins with pencil lead.

Electric Underblanket
Generally used for preheating the bed, it must be switched off before getting in. In order to stop it from creasing, secure the blanket to the mattress. It should have a safety check every two years. Never use in conjunction with a hot water bottle.

Electrical Cables
Keep electrical cables tidy by winding them into a loop and slipping them inside a long cardboard tube.

Embroidery
Before ironing a heavily embroidered item, lay a thick piece of soft material over the ironing board, then lay the item face down and iron it. This will ensure that the raised surface of the embroidery doesn't get crushed.

Enamel Cookware
Use plastic utensils on enamel cookware as metal ones will scratch the enamel.

Extractor Fans
An extractor fan should be installed in a window which

does not open, and opposite the door thereby ensuring air is drawn across the room. Make sure you keep your extractor fan clean and free of grease otherwise it will not work efficiently.

Fabric
To prevent watermarks appearing on fabric when ironing, always press on the wrong side.

To remove a press mark from fabric, hold the garment over a steaming kettle, but keep your hands and face well clear from the steam.

Fat – see also *Sink,* page 54.
If you have accidentally poured hot fat down the sink, immediately pour a pan of very hot water down it; otherwise as soon as the hot fat reaches a cooler temperature it will solidify and cause a blockage.

As soon as hot fat is spilt onto a wooden floor pour cold water over it; this will make the fat solidify and therefore easier to scrape up. Any other marks can be washed away afterwards with hot water and soapless detergent.

Films
Camera films store well at a low temperature in the fridge; heat can cause discolouration of the film. Just keep them dry and away from the back of the fridge where water might drip.

Flies
Flies don't take too kindly to mint. Keep them out of your kitchen by hanging up a basket of mint.

Floor
Stone floors should be cleaned with water containing a small amount of washing soda. (Remember to wear rubber gloves when using washing soda.)

For vinyl floor coverings, use some washing-up liquid and a touch of vinegar.

Floor Mops
After using a floor mop, rinse it thoroughly in a bucket and add several drops of household disinfectant to kill off any lingering bacteria which might be in the mop head.

A sponge floor mop will last longer if stored with its head in a polythene bag.

Flowers, Artificial
Use a hairdryer to get rid of dust from silk flowers.

Freshen up silk flowers – add a touch of your favourite fragrance to their petals.

Freezer
If a power cut should occur, provided that your freezer is well stocked and the door remains shut, food should remain frozen for at least 8 hours and up to 24 hours.

A full freezer functions more efficiently. If your freezer isn't full, fill empty plastic pop bottles half full with water and use these to fill up the spaces.

A freezer should be defrosted at least once a year. Remove food stains on the inside lining with water and some bicarbonate of soda.

Fridge – see *Refrigerator,* page 52.

Frozen Food
Use a clothes peg to reseal opened packets of frozen food.

Frying Pan
The best method of cleaning a frying pan is to run off all the surplus fat, then rinse out thoroughly any remaining

debris under a hot tap.

Furniture – see also *Wood* (DIY Tips, page 133).

Highly polished wood will often fade if subject to bright sunlight. If your table is situated in front of the window, protect it with a heavy blanket or close the curtains when the sun is beating down.

Wash bamboo furniture frequently in salted water, then rinse with clean water. In order to keep it supple and to stop it from splitting, polish occasionally with linseed oil.

Glass

Use a wad of damp cotton wool to pick up broken fragments of glass. Wear protective gloves if necessary and vacuum afterwards to clear up any remaining slivers.

Glasses – for eye glasses see *Spectacles*, page 55.

Separate two glasses stuck one inside the other by filling the inner one with cold water, then immersing both in warm water.

Wash delicate or crystal glasses in warm water with a touch of washing up liquid added. Rinse in clean water, drain and leave to dry on kitchen paper or a tea towel.

Glassware

Never take glassware out of the oven and plunge into cold water; the sudden change in temperature could make it crack.

Hairbrushes

To wash pure hair bristles, dissolve ½ tablespoon of washing soda in some warm water and gently tap the bristles in ensuring the roots don't get wet. Stand the brush on its bristles to dry and away from direct heat. And wear a pair of rubber gloves to protect your hands.

Use a toothpick to dislodge some of the grime from

between the bristles.

Handbags
Leather handbags stuffed with tissue paper will keep their shape when being stored.

Use a vacuum nozzle attachment to clean inside a large handbag.

Hands, Greasy
If the telephone rings and you are in the middle of baking, put your hand into a polythene bag to pick up the telephone.

Hard Water
Remove hard water stains on sinks by rubbing vinegar onto the mark.

Hats
An old grubby-looking pale-coloured straw hat can be revived by cleaning it with an old toothbrush dipped into a solution of 1 tablespoon of lemon juice added to ½ litre (1 pint) of water. Rinse thoroughly and leave to dry outside if possible, but not over direct heat otherwise the straw will crack.

Ice Cubes
If there is an isolated mark on a dry garment dampen the spot with an ice cube before ironing.

Iron
A round-bladed knife, covered with a piece of white cotton material, will remove any residue from the underside of an iron if gently scraped across it. Do this with the iron heated up, but switched off.

Always use distilled water when filling a steam iron. Failure to do so may cause the iron to fur up and in time become faulty.

Remove a sticky patch from the underside of an iron by gently heating it. When it is warm switch off and run the iron back and forwards across a piece of paper sprinkled with salt.

Ironing – see also *Embroidery,* page 39; *Fabric,* page 40; *Knitted Garments,* page 46; *Zip,* page 59.
If you spit on the underside of your iron, the sizzle which it emits will let you know whether the temperature is hot, cold or medium.

To speed up ironing, lay a sheet of aluminium foil, glossy side up, under the ironing board cover. Heat will be reflected back.

Ironing on the right side of a garment will give it a shiny finish; ironing on the wrong side will give a matt finish.

To remove a shiny surface on trousers or a skirt which has occurred after ironing, lay them out flat and wet the area with a clean, wet tea towel. Then lay the damp cloth over and iron gently, lifting the iron on and off. Afterwards, place a sheet of brown paper on the garment and iron over the paper to dry out the garment.

Jam Seals
Waxed paper used in cereal packets is perfect for making jam seals.

Jars
To open a jar lid which is stuck firm, use the old method of pouring hot water over it; failing that, wear a pair of rubber gloves to give a firmer grip when turning the lid.

Jewellery
A coat of clear nail varnish will prevent costume jewellery from tarnishing. If the finish is damaged, it can

often be repaired by rubbing over with a stick of metallic wax (sold for brass rubbings in craft shops), then covering with clear nail varnish.

Jumpers

Before washing jumpers, particularly mohair or angora, turn them inside out, to prevent any bobbling. To remove bobbles from such garments, use the sharp edge of a razor blade to scrape them away very carefully.

Kettle

A piece of sponge placed inside a kettle will prevent it furring up if you live in a hard water area. The scale will be drawn to the sponge instead of to the sides of the kettle.

To remove fur from inside a kettle, fill it with a solution, half vinegar, half water. Boil it, then switch off and leave for about 6 hours, to give the vinegar time to soak through the scale. Rinse the kettle thoroughly several times before using.

Keys

Mark your keys and locks with the same coloured nail varnish or paint. In that way it will be much easier to find the right key.

Kitchen Equipment – see also *Aluminium Pans,* page 32; *Enamel Cookware,* page 39; *Non-stick Pans,* page 49; *Tins, Baking,* page 56.

Metal kitchen graters and pastry cutters can rust easily, so after washing leave them to dry in a warm place, preferably the top of the grill or in a warm oven.

Leaving kitchen knives in a drawer amongst ordinary knives will quickly blunt them.

Keep a stainless steel knife for fruit. Occasionally an ordinary steel knife can react to the acid in the fruit and give a metallic flavour to the fruit.

Knitted Garments
   To press newly washed knitted garments, lay them flat under a chair cushion for several hours.

Labels – see also *Candles*, page 35; *Parcels*, page 50.
   When labelling a parcel, write the name and address on the wrapping and cover with sticky clear tape. If it rains, the address won't streak.

Laminate Worktops
   Bicarbonate of soda applied to a damp cloth will clean marks on laminate worktops.

Lampshades – see *Louvred Doors*, opposite page.

Laundry Basket
   A bin liner secured inside a wicker laundry basket helps prevent clothes snagging on the sides.

Leather Boots
   Rub polish around the wrinkled parts of leather boots to reduce the possibility of their cracking. And if you don't have trees to put inside boots, use rolled up magazines.

Leather Gloves
   Wear leather gloves when washing them, and use either a glove cleaning shampoo or soap flakes (check the washing instructions on the label first). Rinse thoroughly in warm water and hang them outside, away from direct sunlight. When still a little damp put them back on your hands to help regain their shape.

Light Bulbs
   Light bulbs should be cleaned perhaps once a month as a build up of dust over them makes the bulbs overheat. To do this remove them from their sockets (when cool!) and

wipe them over with a piece of cotton wool moistened with methylated spirit. Make sure they are perfectly dry before replacing back into the socket.

Linen
When storing table linen, wrap it in blue tissue paper. White tissue paper lets the light penetrate, which in turn causes yellowing to occur; blue tissue paper offers more protection.

Linseed Oil
When mixed in equal parts with turpentine, linseed oil rubs out water marks from wood.

Both are highly flammable and so should be stored carefully.

Louvred Doors
Use an old blusher brush for cleaning dust out of louvred doors and pleated lampshades.

Matches
Damp matches can be restored so that they light by dipping the igniting end in nail varnish and leaving them to dry.

Mattress Care – see also *Beds, Airing,* page 34.
Keep mattresses clean, turn them regularly, and vacuum both sides using the nozzle attachment of the vacuum cleaner.

Any spilt liquid on a mattress should be dealt with immediately. Stand the mattress on its side and wipe off excess liquid with a clean cloth; dab at the stain with a cloth dipped in cold water. Don't soak the area or it will seep into the filling. Speed up the drying process by using a hair dryer over the area.

Medicine Bottles

Cover the labels on medicine bottles with clear nail varnish to prevent the instructions smearing or fading. A strip of sellotape serves the same purpose.

Methylated Spirit

Methylated spirit is useful for removing many grease stains from various materials (check on a test patch before using). See stain removal tips, page 7. Undiluted it will polish mirrors, jewellery and ivory; used with paraffin it will polish chrome and paintwork. Always keep it stored safely as it is highly inflammable and poisonous.

Mice

To rid a house of unwanted mice, set traps with flour, chocolate or porridge oats. If using poison, situate it in places where young children or animals cannot reach it. The local Environmental Health Office can offer further advice.

Mirrors

To stop a bathroom mirror from steaming up, wipe it over with neat shampoo. Then polish with a clean cloth.

Net Curtains – also known as Lace Curtains.

To allow for shrinkage, leave a good hem when taking up cotton net curtains.

When washing net curtains, fold them into a square and leave to soak overnight in warm soapy water. Gently squeeze out surplus water and spread flat to dry.

The easiest method of drying cotton net is to drip dry until damp, then thread a stair rod along the bottom seam and rehang. This avoids the necessity of ironing. If creasing has occurred, iron whilst the net is still damp.

Repair any small tear in a net curtain with some clear nail varnish.

An old tip for making nets crisp: when freshly washed, dip them into a solution 1 tablespoon sugar and ½ litre (1 pint) water.

Non-stick Pans
Never leave an empty non-stick pan over a lighted gas burner or any other form of heat. Without fat or liquid, the heat will cause the coating on the pan to deteriorate.

Nylon Garments
Wash white nylon on its own, as it often picks up invisible dyes from the water and will quickly turn grey.

Turn a nylon jumper inside out before washing to prevent snags and damage to the outside of the jumper.

Ornaments
Wash china ornaments individually in warm soapy water. Rinse them in hand-hot water and then dry.

Never wash china ornaments which have been broken and then repaired; it could affect the glue. Simply wipe them over with a soft cloth.

Oven (and Hob) – see *Caustic Soda*, page 36.
Clean grubby oven shelves by soaking them overnight in biological detergent and water.

To dispel any lingering smells in an oven, place several pieces of orange peel inside and heat the oven on a low setting for 10 minutes.

If you keep a damp cloth handy then whenever there are any spillages over the hob wipe them up before they can harden. Once a month give the whole thing a good clean down by removing the gas burners and any other parts. A cream cleanser can be used to clean the hob, and a nylon scourer to remove stubborn spots, but never use anything sharp or it will damage the hob.

Use a pipe cleaner to clean the holes on gas burners. The longer they are left the more likely it is they will fill up with grease, thereby diminishing their efficiency.

Paints, Children's
Because glycerine has a softening property, several drops brushed over children's paints will prevent them from drying out and cracking.

Parcels – see also *Candles*, page 35; *Labels*, page 46.
Before tying a parcel, dampen the string. As the string dries, it will shrink around the package, making it more secure.

When sending a parcel overseas, wrap and label it twice; if the outer covering is damaged it should still reach its destination intact.

Pastry Board
Clean a pastry board quickly by sprinkling it liberally with salt and rubbing it over with the palm of your hand to loosen any remaining bits of pastry. Wash and rinse as usual.

Pet's Bowl
To prevent a dog/cat's dish from sliding on the floor during feeding, stick a piece of self-adhesive foam draught-excluder under it.

Picture
To cure a "crooked" picture, wrap a small piece of adhesive tape around the highest point of the wire – this will prevent the picture slipping sideways.

Pillow
When buying a pillow, hold it at one end and shake. If the bulk of the filling falls down to the opposite end, the pillow will go flat after a while.

Plastic Bags
Store plastic bags in the freezer to stop them sticking together.

Plunger – see also *Sink*, page 54.
Blocked sink and no plunger? Then use a thick sponge, this should have the desired effect.

Quarry Tiles
Use red tile polish on a red quarry tiled doorstep as it withstands the heavy amount of traffic far better than red tile seal.

Quilt Covers
Feather and down quilts should be cleaned professionally.

Radiator
Use an old sock secured around a piece of garden bamboo to clean behind a radiator.

Radio Station
Indicate your favourite stations by fixing sticky cut-out triangle shapes onto the radio.

Raincoat
Wash a nylon raincoat in warm suds. Rinse thoroughly and drip dry. If a nylon raincoat is creased badly, it can be ironed over with a warm iron.

Razor Blades
When not in use, place your razor in a mug which is half full of water and a teaspoon of borax. The borax prevents rust and soap congealing along the edge of the blade.

Records
Any records which are slightly warped should be placed in between two clean sheets of glass and stored in a warm

airing cupboard. The heat and pressure should correct the problem.

Refrigerator
Clean a refrigerator with warm water to which is added a teaspoon of bicarbonate of soda.

If there is a smell inside, put a piece of charcoal at the back of a shelf, or a crumpled newspaper, but make sure you change them regularly.

Keep all goods well covered as smells from foods tend to permeate.

Speed up defrosting the fridge by placing a bowl of boiling water on the bottom, or hold a hair dryer outside the fridge and direct the hot air into it.

Rubber Gloves
Extend the life of rubber gloves, by rinsing them after use; then hang up to dry. To stop sharp nails from splitting the finger ends, push small pieces of cotton wool into the finger tips.

Rubber Mat
If a rubber mat has gone hard, soak it in a bath of warm water topping up occasionally so that an even temperature is maintained. Leave it steeping for an hour then rub dry.

Rubber Sheeting
Wash rubber sheeting, which may be used for covering a bed mattress, in warm soapy water, rinse well and dry with an old towel. Dust with french chalk to give extra protection. When storing, roll it around a broom handle and leave in a well ventilated cupboard (not an airing cupboard). Never fold up or the rubber will perish.

Saucepans – see *Aluminium Pans*, page 32.

Scissors
Sharpen scissors by cutting across a metal knitting needle several times, an alternative is to cut across a bottle neck top.

Sheets
Prevent sheets and light garments tangling up on the washing line by clipping pegs along their bottom edge to hold them down.

Shoe, Leather or Suede
To condition leather shoes, rub baby oil into them last thing at night – rub off in the morning.

Stuff wet leather shoes with newspaper. Leave to dry in a natural heat.

Revive shabby looking suede shoes by steaming them over a boiling kettle, but make sure you don't scald your hands.

Shoe, Coloured
Conceal a scuff mark on a shoe by dipping a cloth into paint (the same colour as the shoe) and applying the paint over the spot. Leave to dry and then polish. Or hide the mark using a felt tipped marker pen.

Shoe, Fabric
Fabric shoes often respond well to a quick wash in the machine, but make sure afterwards they are stuffed with newspaper or shoe trees when drying, to get their shape back.

Shoe, Slingback
Stick a piece of adhesive draught excluder inside the strap of a pair of slingback shoes if they keep falling down.

Shoe Brushes
To clean them: stand the brush, bristles downwards,

into some white spirit. Pat the brush up and down in the spirit, then stand it on some thick newspaper to drain. Rinse with water and washing up liquid. Then drain again.

Shoe Polish
Soften hard shoe polish by adding a few drops of olive oil or turpentine into it. Alternatively, place the tin in a warm oven for a couple of minutes.

Shower Curtain – see also *Bath*, page 33.
Clean the build-up of soap on a shower curtain by soaking the curtains in warm water with some water softener added.

To prevent mildew appearing on shower curtains soak the curtains in salt water before using, and after each time they are washed.

Sink – see also *Fat*, page 40; *Hard Water*, page 43; *Plunger,* page 51; *Taps,* page 56; *Wash Basins,* page 57.
Pour a handful of washing soda and hot water down the kitchen sink once a week to keep its drain unblocked. Remember to wear rubber gloves when using washing soda.

Smells – see also *Oven*, page 49; *Refrigerator,* page 52.
After cooking kippers, remove the fishy odour from the pan by emptying tea leaves into it. Cover with water and leave for 5–10 minutes, rinse and wash. To dispel the strong onion smell from a wooden chopping board, cover it with coarse salt and then rinse under cold water.

To remove the onion smell from hands, wash them as quickly as possible with cold water (warm water seals the smell). If it still lingers, massage lemon juice into your hands and then wash with soap and water.

Soap
Soap will last longer if stored in a warm, dry place such

as the airing cupboard and kept in its wrapper.

Soap Dish
Scrub a soap dish with a mild solution of washing soda and very hot water. Remember to wear rubber gloves to protect your hands from the washing soda.

Spectacles
When painting, cover each lens with some clingfilm to keep it paint-free.

For streak-free spectacles, put a drop of vinegar on your cloth when cleaning.

Steel Wool
Store steel wool in a jar of soapy water to prevent it from turning rusty.

Suitcases
When storing a suitcase, add a bar of soap to keep it smelling fresh.

Swimsuits
Always soak a swimsuit after use in cold water to extract any remains of salt and chlorine. Wash then dry.

Table Mats
To keep cloth table mats flat when not being used, hang them up on a clipboard.

If cork mats are ingrained with stains, rub them with fine sandpaper. If the stains are damp, try rubbing with a wet pumice stone. Remove the loose powder with a damp cloth and then pat dry.

Tablets
To crush tablets, place then in a teaspoon and then press another teaspoon down on top of them.

Tape Measure
Revive a limp tape measure by ironing it between two waxed sheets of paper.

Taps
Clean behind taps with an old toothbrush dipped in bath cleaner.

Teapot
To clean a stained teapot spout, pack full of damp salt; leave overnight; wash thoroughly with boiling water the following day.

Tights
When drying tights on the washing line, put a coin in each foot to prevent entanglement. Blow dry tights should they be needed in a hurry.

Tins, Baking
To prevent rust occurring in tins, make sure they are dried off thoroughly and then popped into a warm oven. Should the tins be exceptionally greasy or dirty, add some washing soda to the boiling water, wash and dry.

Store baking tins in a warm dry cupboard to prevent moisture from weakening the seams or causing rust.

Toothpaste
To make sure all remnants of toothpaste are used up, secure a clothes peg on the end and roll it up tightly.

Use toothpaste to fix posters temporarily to the wall.

Umbrella
Patch up a hole in an umbrella by fixing a small piece of matching nylon on the inside with clear adhesive.

Vacuum Cleaner Bags
Add a handful of dried herbs into a new vacuum cleaner

bag; the aroma will freshen rooms each time you vacuum.

Vacuum Flask
To clean a vacuum flask, crush an eggshell and drop it into the flask, adding some hot water; shake the flask, then leave overnight to soak. Alternatively, soak the flask with a solution of soda in boiling water. Rinse thoroughly the following day. In order to prevent mould, store the flask with the cap off.

Vase
Prevent dust gathering in the neck of a long vase by plugging with cotton wool. The dust will then gather on top of the cotton wool and can be removed whenever the vase is washed.

Venetian Blinds
Wear old socks, one on either hand, when cleaning venetian blinds. Use one to wash and the other to dry.

Clean venetian blinds with an anti-static polish and they will remain clean longer.

Vomit
A quick squirt from a soda syphon will help to get rid of the smell from carpets once the vomit has been cleaned up.

Wash Basins – see also *Sink,* page 54.
Wipe ceramic wash basins daily with a mild soap solution, rinse and dry.

Washing – see also *Acrylic Garments,* page 32; *Angora,* page 33; *Dresses,* page 38; *Jumpers,* page 45; *Laundry Basket,* page 46; *Net Curtains,* page 48; *Nylon Garments,* page 49; *Sheets,* page 53; *Tights,* page 56; *Wool,* page 59.
Prevent clothes from freezing on the washing line when cold by adding a handful of salt to the rinsing water.

When hand washing dusters, add several drops of paraffin to the final rinse – furniture will polish up beautifully.

Before washing a new garment, soak in salt and water to prevent colours running.

Put delicate garments which require washing into a pillow case. Secure by tying an old nylon stocking around it, and pop it into the washing machine on a gentle wash.

Fabric softener added to a final rinse helps reduce any static in the garment.

For extra soft jumpers when hand washing, add a capful of cream hair rinse conditioner to the final rinse.

Remove any collar tidemarks by rubbing the area with a little undiluted washing-up liquid before washing.

Washing Soda
Extremely handy to have in the cupboard as it has many uses: as a water softener; it's ideal for cleaning drains, etc.; but always wear gloves when using.

Windows
To stop windows misting up, wipe them with a cloth dipped in half methylated spirit and half glycerine.

To stop a car windscreen from freezing over on icy mornings, rub it over with half a potato.

If the wipers fail, cut a potato in half and run the cut end up and down the windscreen. This will prevent any water droplets from forming. If travelling a long distance then frequent rerubbing is required.

Wood – see *Furniture*, page 42; *Linseed Oil*, page 47.

Wool

Great care is required when washing and handling a pure wool garment in order to maintain its qualities. Don't rub wool garments or pull them around too much as they could lose their shape.

To reduce the risk of shrinking, wash and rinse wool in water of the same temperature. Remove the garment from the water gently, making sure no part of it pulls or it will stretch.

If a garment has shrunk, soak it in warm water mixed with some hair shampoo. This may soften the fabric sufficiently to reshape it.

Don't dry white or light coloured woollens in direct sunlight; it could turn them yellow.

A teaspoon of glycerine added to rinsing water will help keep woollen garments soft.

If you don't have a spin dryer, roll the garment up in a towel and gently squeeze. Surplus water will then be absorbed by the towel.

Ensure all soap is rinsed clear from woollens by adding one tablespoon of vinegar to the rinsing water.

Prevent cuffs on woollens going baggy when washing: wrap a rubber band around them and fold back.

Keep woollen blankets soft and fluffy by adding a teaspoon of olive oil to the final rinse.

Zips

If a zip fastener doesn't run smoothly, shake some talcum powder over it; failing that run a pencil along its teeth.

When ironing a garment with a zip, slip a length of foam

rubber inside the garment, this will prevent the iron from creating creases.

3

COSMETIC HINTS

Allergy Testing
A simple way to determine whether or not you may be allergic to a certain cosmetic: dampen an area of skin along your inner arm with tepid water. Apply the cosmetic you think you might be allergic to and leave it in place for 24 hours. If, after this length of time, there is some reaction, i.e. itchiness or redness, this indicates that your skin may be allergic to this cosmetic.

Baby Shampoo – see also *Hair,* page 66.
Don't apply shampoo onto a baby's scalp without first warming it up a little by rubbing it between your hands.

Bath Time
Because soap and water dry out the skin, make sure after having a bath you moisturise your skin. Or, add a splash of bath oil to the bath water – it helps prevent skin from drying out.

Bikini Line
Before shaving the bikini line, cover it with a towel soaked in hot water. Leave it on for five minutes allowing the hair to soften and make shaving less uncomfortable.

Blusher
Blusher is used to accentuate features in the face so when buying it choose one several shades darker than

your skin colour.

Broken Ends – see also *Hair*, page 66.
Broken/split ends in hair cannot be cured, in time they will only run up the rest of the hair strand – the only remedy is to get a good haircut.

Brushing
Never use a brush on wet hair, it will only tear it; instead use a wide-toothed comb.

Concealer
Concealer is ideal for small areas on your face which need covering, such as a spot, a pimple, dark circles, etc. Buy one a little lighter than your skin tone.

Conditioning
When conditioning your hair, concentrate on the oldest sections, i.e. the ends. If you have run out of conditioner, try adding a splash of vinegar to the final rinse; result – a shiny head of hair.

Cuticles
Cuticles play an extremely important job in that they protect the base of the nail where growth occurs. Before pushing them back, warm up some hand lotion and soak the nails in it for several minutes; this will make the job of pushing the cuticles back easier.

Dandruff
If you suffer with dandruff: always rinse your hair thoroughly several times after each wash; use a medicated shampoo and, before drying, apply some witch hazel along the scalp.

Dry Hair
Olive oil once a month is the perfect treatment for dry hair. After massaging it well into the hair, cover your head with a hot towel and leave for several hours to give it time

Fig. 2. Olive Oil Treatment
   A woman's head covered with a towel.

to work. Then shampoo hair as normal. Don't try rinsing the oil off before adding the shampoo: oil and water just don't mix and the oil would stay firm. Instead, apply the shampoo and massage it into the head well before adding water; rinse your hair several times.

Dry Shampoo
   In between washing your hair, freshen it up by rubbing cologne-soaked balls of cotton wool into the scalp.

Drying Hair
   Never blow dry hair when it is wet; intense heat for a long period of time only encourages broken ends. Instead, towel dry as much as possible, then blow dry.

Elbows
   The skin around elbows is often dry so give it a regular treatment with moisturising cream.

Eye Liner

An eye liner pencil should simply float over the skin. If yours is a little too firm, soften the end by running it under some hot water for several seconds. Wait until it has cooled before using.

Eye Make-up Remover – see also *Make-up*, page 68.

Whether using a commercially bought make-up remover or one you have made up yourself, always leave it in place for 30 seconds or so. This will give the make-up a chance to soften and therefore make it easier to remove. For a cheap eye make-up remover, warm some petroleum jelly until it is runny and then apply this over the eyes; remove with a piece of cotton wool.

Eye Shadows

If eye shadow doesn't stay on, put baby/face powder over each lid and then apply the eye shadow. The powder will give the eye shadow a firm non-greasy base on which to stick.

For an eye shadow that will remain on throughout the day, use a powder one. Before applying, stick the applicator into some water and then into the eye shadow.

Eyebrows

Before plucking eyebrows, lay a hot flannel over the area for several minutes to open the pores and make plucking the hairs a little easier.

Petroleum jelly brushed daily through the eyebrows with a toothbrush will help maintain their shape.

Eyelashes

Eyelashes will appear thicker if baby/face powder is patted over them before applying mascara.

Eyes

To reduce puffy eyes, dip two metal spoons into a glass

of iced water. Lay a small piece of thin cotton material over each eye, then place a spoon over this and leave for several minutes.

To relax tired, aching eyes, place either a piece of

Fig. 3 Tired Eyes
Relax by placing a piece of cucumber over each eye.

cucumber over each, or a cold, wet teabag, for 10 minutes or so.

For deep-set eyes, use lots of mascara and, to make the eyes look larger, apply blue eye liner along the inside lower lid.

Face Powder
Make sure your face powder remains on throughout the day by applying it firmly onto the skin with a piece of cotton wool.

Feet
Treat dry skin on feet with a pumice stone. Glycerine rubbed on at night will help to soften hard, dry skin.

Go around barefoot and relax tired feet. Another good tip is to soak your feet for a good 15 minutes, in a bowl of warm water with salt added.

Dust talcum powder over bare feet during hot, sticky weather and they are less likely to cling to sandals.

A little baking soda sprinkled in shoes and left overnight will absorb any lingering odours!

Foundation
A few drops of moisturiser added to foundation will make it easier to apply.

For a better finish, apply foundation with a slightly damp sponge.

Another tip: don't buy foundation which is too watery, otherwise it will leave streaky lines over your face. It should have the consistency of thick cream.

Greasy Hair
If you have greasy hair, comb it. Don't brush it. Brushing encourages the sebaceous glands to secrete more oil.

Hair – see also *Broken Ends,* page 62; *Brushing,* page 62; *Conditioning,* page 63; *Dandruff,* page 63; *Dry Hair,* page 62; *Drying Hair,* page 63; *Greasy Hair,* above.
For shiny hair, rinse it in cold water after washing.

If you haven't time to wash your hair, freshen it up by dabbing the roots with cotton wool soaked in cologne.

When washing youngsters' hair, prevent shampoo

running into their eyes, by smearing a band of petroleum jelly over their foreheads.

Pipe cleaners make great ponytail grips.

Hairspray
For a natural finish to your hairstyle, put hairspray onto the brush and then run it over your hair.

Hands – see also *Lemon*, below.
For soft silky hands after gardening or other manual work, put a small amount of cooking oil in your palms, sprinkle with ordinary sugar and rub them together. Wash as usual.

Jewellery
Always put perfume on *before* jewellery, otherwise the components in the perfume may cause a film to appear over the jewellery.

Legs
A high-cut swimsuit makes legs look longer.

Before shaving legs, smooth baby oil over them. Result: smooth, silky legs. You can also use cooking oil to achieve this.

Lemon
A lemon has many uses in the cosmetic world; nails which are marked with vegetable juice can be bleached with lemon juice; it may be used as a hair lightener; and if hands are particularly smelly a quick rub over with a lemon will often work wonders!

Lip Pencil
Lip pencils and other cosmetic pencils will be easier to sharpen if popped into the fridge for about 15 minutes.

Lips
Bright lipstick makes the mouth appear larger; the

opposite will occur if muted colours are worn.

To narrow down full lips, use a lip pencil which is several shades darker than the lipstick and apply inside the line.

Because lips have no oil glands, they are very suscept-ible to becoming dry and chapped. So keep them well moisturised with a light coating of petroleum jelly.

Lipstick
Outline lips with a brush or lip pencil to make a neat job of applying lipstick. In hot weather, lipsticks can be stored in the fridge to prevent them melting.

Make-up
Lighten base make-up with a touch of moisturiser.

The maximum shelf life for eye cosmetics is generally one year. But if eyes tend to be sensitive, it may be advisable to replace them every three months.

Manicure
A quick way to dry freshly polished nails is to dip them into a bowl of iced water.

Mascara
When applying mascara always do so in downward (and upward) strokes; applying it side-to-side will result in the lashes joining together.

Nail Varnish
Store nail varnish in the fridge and it won't thicken. Before required, remove from the fridge and stand it upside down for 35 minutes; shake gently before using.

By adding several drops of nail varnish remover, the varnish will go further.

Rub the neck of the bottle with some petroleum jelly before putting the top on to make the nail varnish bottle easier to open next time.

Nails – see also *Cuticles,* page 62; *Lemon,* page 67; *Manicure,* page, 68.
Press nails into some petroleum jelly if you are about to do a messy job to stop dirt becoming lodged.

Nicotine-stained fingers can be cleaned if rubbed occasionally with smoker's toothpaste.

Weak nails are better kept short and well filed. To strengthen them, use extra hardening varnish.

Perfume – see also *Jewellery,* page 67.
Ensure perfume lingers by applying some petroleum jelly before the perfume.

Shaving – see *Bikini Line,* page 61; *Legs,* page 67.

Sun Cream
Any sun cream left over from your summer holiday can be used as a body lotion if you don't want to keep it until next year. Once opened, sun cream deteriorates and loses its protective qualities but retains its moisturising abilities.

For extra protection during summer, choose a foundation cream containing a sun cream.

Teeth
A toothbrush should have soft bristles. Soften those which are too hard by holding them under hot water. Firm up soft ones under running cold water.

Baking soda makes a good substitute if you have run out of toothpaste.

4
KNITTING AND SEWING HINTS

Anoraks
Don't throw an old anorak away, especially if the body is okay. Simply remove the arms, sew some binding around the armholes and use as a padded waistcoat.

Bobbins
Keep all sewing bobins together by threading them onto

Fig. 4 Knitting needles with cotton bobbins on and a cork on the pointed end.

a knitting needle and securing a cork or cotton wool ball at the pointed end to stop them sliding off.

Button
To make sure four-holed buttons stay firm, sew each pair of holes separately; then at least if one side becomes loose the other side will keep the button in place until you can find a needle!

To strengthen buttons on delicate garments, cut a small piece of material of similar colour and lay this on the inside behind the button. Then sew through all thicknesses.

Keep buttons and other small objects away from babies and young children – they could swallow them.

Buttonholes
Ensure newly made buttonholes won't split by overstitching around them.

Casting Off – see also *Knitting*, page 73.
When casting off a garment use larger needles for a more pliable finish.

Casting On – see also *Knitting*, page 73.
If casting on a lot of stitches, slip in a coloured thread at intervals to make the recounting process less tedious.

Children's Clothes – see *Hemming*, page 72.

Cotton Thread
A touch of hairspray sprayed onto the end of cotton thread will stiffen it and make it easier to thread.

Curtains
When making curtains, sew a small weight along the seams every so often, and also at the corners, to keep them weighted down.

Cushion Stuffing
When stuffing cushions with small bits of plastic foam, pop in several larger pieces to stop them all from settling down at one end.

Dropped Stitches
Use a crochet hook for picking up dropped stitches when knitting.

Elastic

When threading elastic through a casing, attach a small safety pin to each end. Pin one end onto the garment and thread the other through.

If replacing elastic, sew the new piece onto the end of the old one and as you pull the old one out from the other end the new one is threaded into place.

Thin shirring elastic is useful for stitching into ribbed parts of a knitted garment to ensure they don't lose their shape. You can either knit the elastic in, or alternatively sew it in place once the garment is complete.

Fabric – see also *Looped Fabrics,* page 74.

Use hair grips when hemming a fine fabric garment; pins will leaven an unsightly mark.

When pinning slippery fabric such as nylon, stick the pins into some soap beforehand to ensure that they get a better grip. Also, secure slippery fabric in place on your table with pieces of sticky tape.

Fair Isle

When knitting a Fair Isle garment, colour in codings relating to the various coloured wools on the pattern; this makes it much easier to follow.

Hemming

A length of string secured between two chairs at the required height makes a perfect hemline marker. Cover the string with chalk then tie it between the chairs. Put the garment on, then turn slowly around and ensure the garment touches the string all the way round.

Before storing a child's summer dress away, unpick the hem and iron it. Next summer, when adjusting the hem to fit, there will no unsightly hem marks needing camouflage. Also, when taking up the hems on a child's dress or trousers, use iron-on-tape; as the child grows, the hems can be let down without leaving any unsightly marks. Usually after several washes you can pull the old tape off.

Invisible Stitch
To make an invisible stitch when knitting, pick up a loop in between the two needles and work into the back of it.

Jeans
If you want to prevent frayed bottom edges on jeans, sew bias binding around the inside of the hems to take the brunt of the water.

When patching jeans, stitch up the hip pocket, turn the jeans inside out and use the redundant pocket for the patch.

Jersey
When sewing jersey, a needle with a rounded end is far gentler than a pointed one. A sharp pointed one can easily cause the material to ladder.

Joins
A jumper with many coloured threads will look much neater if the strands are woven tidily into the back of the garment.

Knitting – see also *Casting Off,* page 71; *Casting On,* page 71; *Dropped Stitches,* page 71; *Invisible Stitch,* above; *Sewing Up,* page 76.
Give a more elasticated edge to a knitted garment by using larger needles when casting on and off.

It's quicker when knitting sleeves to work them both at the same time; the shaping and pattern need only be worked out once.

If you suffer from sweaty palms, when knitting rub some talcum powder over them.

Knitting Needles
For people with arthritic hands, wooden or bamboo knitting needles are warmer and lighter to use than the traditional metal ones.

Wool will slide more easily along the needles if they are occasionally rubbed with some spray polish on a cloth.

Knitting Wool
If you want to re-knit unpicked yarn, wind it tightly around a stiff piece of cardboard, dip it into some tepid water and then leave to dry out thoroughly.

Lining
Use the old lining as a pattern when making a new lining for a garment.

Looped Fabrics
To stop terry towelling and other such material becoming tangled in the foot of the sewing machine, lay a sheet of tissue paper over the material before you start sewing; when finished it can be torn away.

Mohair
Put mohair in the refrigerator for an hour before using and it will be easier to knit.

Don't wash mohair too often. Frequent washing causes it to fur up.

Needles – see also *Pins,* opposite page.
Keep sewing needles safely together by threading them through some paper.

Before sewing stiff material, run your needle through a piece of soap and the material will be easier to penetrate.

Nylon – see *Fabric*, page 72.

Pattern – see also *Fair Isle,* page 72; *Lining,* page 74.
Make sure you don't lose your place when working from a knitting pattern, by marking or highlighting the size you are knitting, throughout the pattern.

Pin Cushions
Dried coffee beans make an ideal filling for home made pin cushions, or for the same effect with less expense, you could use rice or dried peas, beans or barley.

Pinking Shears
To neaten edges of garments on which the material won't fray, use pinking shears.

Pins – see also *Fabric*, page 72.
Keep pins and needles neatly in your sewing basket by sticking them in a piece of foam. Never leave them where babies and children could play with them or where anyone might accidently step on them.

Plastic
If sewing plastic, put it between greaseproof paper. Not only will this prevent the plastic from slipping around, it will also make any matching up with markings on the underneath garment easier to see. After the sewing is complete, simply tear the paper away.

Polo Necks
Finish off the remaining couple of centimetres on a polo neck sweater on larger needles – the shape and look will be better.

PVC
Dust PVC with talcum powder before machine sewing to stop it from sticking.

When sewing with PVC, use paper clips instead of pins.

Scissors
Keep dressmaking scissors for cutting out fabric only. If you use them on paper they'll soon go blunt.

Seams
Prevent a seam above the split on a straight skirt from splitting any higher by sewing a large button at the bottom of the seam on the inside.

Use eyebrow tweezers to extract redundant pieces of cotton left in the seams.

Sewing Machines – see also *Looped Fabrics*, page 74; *PVC*, page 75.
Use a pastry brush to remove fluff from awkward parts of a sewing machine.

Sewing Up
When sewing up a knitted garment, backstitch is often preferable, especially over the shoulders, as it gives a firmer hold.

Sleeves – see *Knitting*, page 73.

Slip Stitch
Always slip the first stitch of each knit line for a neater edge to your work.

Stitch Holder
If you haven't a safety pin for a stitch holder, use a pipe cleaner. Just slip it through and twist the ends together.

Stocking Stitch
Prevent stocking stitch knitting from rolling up by purling the stitch at each end of every knit row.

Tailor's Chalk
An odd piece of soap is a useful substitute for tailor's chalk.

Templates

Use stiffened interlining as patchwork templates instead of card. They can also be used in place of heavy backing.

5

COOKING HINTS

Almond Paste
Before putting almond paste onto a fruit cake, warm up
some apricot jam and apply this to the top. The jam will
improve the adherence of the paste to the cake, and,
because it is less tangy than other jams, will in no way
impair the flavour of the cake.

Almonds
To skin almonds quickly and effectively, boil them for
several minutes, drain then plunge into cold water;
seconds later the skins will slide off.

Angelica
To remove some of the sugar from angelica (if you want
to), pop it in a bowl of hot water for a few minutes; drain
and dry well.

Apples
Before baking apples in the oven, make a cross around
the top to prevent them from exploding out of their skins.

For ready-to-use apple sauce, freeze stewed apple in ice
cube trays.

Apricots
When buying apricots choose those which feel firm and
which have clear skins.

To stone apricots cut them in half, twist the two halves in opposite directions, then use the tip of a knife to remove the stone.

Artichokes
Because Jerusalem artichokes are awkward to peel, choose the smoothest looking ones.

When buying globe artichokes pick the green ones with tightly packed leaves.

When cooking globe artichokes, enhance their flavour by adding a few drops of vinegar to the salted water.

Asparagus
To revive sad looking asparagus stand it upright in a jug with some water, cover with a plastic bag to keep the air out, and leave in the fridge for half an hour before cooking.

When opening a can of asparagus tips do so at the bottom end, thereby protecting the tops which contain much of the goodness.

Aubergines
Aubergines do not often need skinning but if you prefer them skinned, grill them until the skins turn black and can be peeled off.

Aubergines tend to taste a little bitter, so, to extract some of this bitterness, slice them, sprinkle some salt over and leave for an hour. Rinse thoroughly with cold water, then dry.

Avocados
To test whether an avocado is ripe squeeze the narrow end: it should feel slightly soft.

Bacon
When cooking bacon with rind, snip into the edges to stop it rolling up.

Batter
Batter may be prepared well before it is required and left at room temperature for at least four hours (in the fridge up to 24 hours). Extra liquid may be required to restore it to its original consistency.

Beef
If you prefer your joint eaten cold it will carve better if left to stand for 10 minutes after removing it from the oven.

Beetroot
If cooking raw beetroot, retain the long root otherwise the beetroot will bleed into the water and lose its colour and some of its goodness. Do not damage the skin at all; twist the leaves off.

Bilberries
Enhance the delicate flavour of bilberries by adding a squeeze of lemon juice to them.

Biscuits
Keep biscuits fresh in the biscuit tin by adding one or two sugar lumps. The sugar will absorb any moisture and keep the biscuits crisp.

Before cutting biscuit mixture, dip the cutter into some flour which will stop any pastry sticking to it.

Blackcurrants
A simple method to detach blackcurrants from their stalks is to open freeze them; before thawing give them a good shake and most of the fruit will drop off. Run the prongs of a fork through the stems of those that don't.

Brazil Nuts

To shell brazil nuts, store them in the freezer for several hours. When they come out they will crack open far easier.

Bread – see also *Rolls,* page 100.

Use stale fruit loaf as a base for tasty bread and butter pudding.

To warm up bread buns, pop them into a damp paper bag and into a moderate oven for 5 minutes.

Fresh bread will cut better if chilled in the freezer for 5 minutes.

Broccoli

Broccoli doesn't keep very well so it is best used within a day of purchase unless it is well wrapped. Buy broccoli with small crisp-looking heads.

Brussels Sprouts

Choose Brussels sprouts with tightly packed heads and bright green in colour. When cooking them never put on the saucepan lid, otherwise they will smell.

Butter

Use a potato peeler to make butter curls; make sure the butter is firm but not too hard.

To soften up butter for baking, pop it into the microwave on defrost for 35 seconds.

Dip a whisk into boiling water; it helps to melt butter which is too cold to cream.

Cakes

You will know that a cake is cooked when, after being gently pressed in the middle, it rises up. Another sure sign is if a skewer comes out from the middle of the cake clean.

Before creaming fat and sugar together, stand the mixing bowl in some hot water; the heat will make it easier to cream.

Canned Fruit
Take canned fruit out of the tin if storing it in the fridge, otherwise the taste of the fruit will be impaired.

Carrots
Store carrots in a cool dark place and always remove any plastic covering; failure to do so will cause the carrots to sweat and deteriorate. Unwashed carrots keep better than those washed.

Cauliflower
When boiling cauliflower leave the lid off, otherwise it will smell. Retain its whiteness by adding a few drops of milk/lemon juice to the water.

Celery
To revive limp celery, wrap it in some newspaper and stand it upright in a jug of iced water for half an hour before required.

Cheese
Wrap cheese in kitchen foil when storing in the fridge. Remove from the fridge and unwrap an hour before serving, to enhance the flavour.

Cheesecake
To remove a non-cook cheesecake from the tin without its breaking, line the base and around the sides with aluminium foil, using the excess foil as handles. A loose bottomed cake tin or flan dish can also be used as long as it is well greased before adding the cheesecake mixture.

Cherries
Before adding glacé cherries to a recipe, wash them until all trace of the sugary syrup has gone – it is the syrup

which causes them to sink to the bottom of the cake.

Chicken
A safe way to defrost a frozen chicken is to remove it from its plastic packaging and lay it on the grill rack, allowing the liquid to drip into the tray. Whilst thawing, cover the chicken with a sheet of aluminium foil. To reduce the risk of food poisoning, remember, raw meat should never be stored close to or above cooked meat. There are certain live organisms in raw meat which are killed off by the cooking process.

Chocolate
The best way to melt chocolate is by breaking it into pieces and placing in a bowl over a pan of gently simmering water.

A darker appearance can be given to chocolate cake if the tin is dusted with cocoa instead of flour.

Christmas Cake
To keep the top of your Christmas cake soft, sprinkle water over before putting it into the oven.

To add brandy or whisky to your Christmas cake after it has cooked: turn the cake upside down and make holes in the bottom with a skewer, pour in the brandy/whisky and leave to soak through.

Coconut
If a coconut is in good condition you will hear the milk sloshing round inside. To get the milk out, pierce two of the three eyes with a sharp implement.

Coffee
Ground coffee will retain its flavour longer if it is securely wrapped and stored in the fridge.

Cornflakes
Crisp up soggy cornflakes by popping them on a baking sheet and into a warm oven for 10 minutes.

Cream – see also *Whipping Cream,* page 103.
When whisking up cream in hot weather, chill the bowl, the whisks and the cream!

Cucumber
Store cucumber in a cool dry place and keep the cut end covered with foil. This will prevent the air turning it soft.

Curry
When stirring curries use a metal spoon: wooden ones can often get stained by the spices.

Stir in some natural yoghurt to cool down a very hot curry.

Deep Frying
To test whether cooking oil is at the correct temperature for frying, drop a cube of bread into the hot oil: if it turns brown within 30 seconds or so it is ready. Make sure food is dry before adding to the oil; cold liquid meeting with hot fat will spit which is dangerous.

Dried Fruit
To enhance the flavour of dried prunes or figs, soak them in some leftover tea and cook them in the same liquid.

Boiling water poured over dried apple will cause it to absorb the water and swell up.

Store dried fruit in airtight containers and put them in a cool dry place.

Duck

Before roasting duck, pierce the skin with a sharp fork to release some of the fat, then for a crisp skin smother it with salt. For a lovely golden skin follow the same procedure, and about ten minutes before the duck is cooked melt a tablespoon of clear honey and brush this over the surface.

Easter Eggs

Easter time means decorating hard boiled eggs. To give eggs colour: onion skins wrapped around during boiling will give them an orange colour; boiling with beetroot will turn them red.

Eggs

Stop a boiling egg from cracking by piercing the round end with a pin. As it cooks, the air which builds up inside

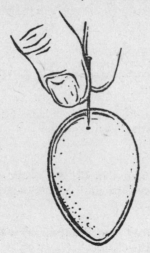

Fig. 5 An egg being pierced by a pin before boiling it.

will seep through the hole instead of pushing out and causing the shell to crack.

Shell a freshly hard boiled egg under running water.

To keep eggs separate when frying, place metal pastry cutters in the frying pan and crack the eggs into them.

For perfectly poached eggs put a touch of vinegar in with the boiling water; it helps the egg to solidify.

Never boil eggs straight from the fridge. The sudden change in temperature will make them crack. Put them into tepid water and bring to the boil gently.

There are many ingenious methods of separating yolks from whites but here is a simple one to try. Crack the egg onto a plate and cover the yolk with an eggcup, then tip the plate to allow the egg white to fall into a cup.

Hard boiled eggs are easier to cut if the blade of the knife is wet.

Fat – see also *Margarine,* page 93.
Add a little bit of flour when frying; not only will it absorb excess moisture, it will also stop fat from spitting.

Grease tins with lard or vegetable fat; because they contain no water or salt, the contents are less likely to stick to the tin.

Fish
When buying fresh fish check that its eyes and skin both shine, that the gills are a rich pink colour, and that it has a healthy sea-fish smell about it.

For a firmer grip when skinning fish dip your fingers in salt beforehand.

For extra crispy fish batter add 15ml (1 tbsp) of vinegar to the mixture.

Flour

When coating meat, put the flour and the meat into a polythene bag. Give a gentle shake to distribute the flour evenly. Throw the bag away when finished.

Fruit – see also *Canned Fruit,* page 82; *Dried Fruit,* page 84.

Many pale fruits such as bananas and apples quickly discolour once cut open, due to the reaction of the fruit's substances with the air. Prevent this happening by brushing lemon juice over the fruit.

Fruit Cake – see also *Almond Paste,* page 78.

If the top of your fruit cake seems to be browning too quickly, cover it with a double sheet of greaseproof paper.

Fruit Juices

Once a carton of fruit juice is opened, store it in the fridge and reseal the pack as much as possible. Air only hastens deterioration of the juice.

Freeze fruit juice and leftover syrup into ice cubes – tasty when added to various drinks.

Frying – see *Deep Frying,* page 84; *Fat,* page opposite.

Fudge

For perfectly shaped pieces of fudge pour the mixture into ice cube trays and leave to set. If the trays are plastic, allow the fudge to cool a little before doing this, or the trays may melt!

Garlic

When peeling garlic cloves, lay a flat-bladed knife over the clove and slam down hard. But keep fingers clear!

Glaze

Melted honey poured over lamb makes a delicious caramel glaze.

Gooseberries
To top and tail gooseberries, rub them both ways down a cheese grater.

Large, plump, firm gooseberries taste far sweeter than smaller ones.

Grapefruit
Warm up a grapefruit in the microwave on a low setting for one minute – you will get more juice.

Before cutting a grapefruit, roll it between your hands. Then take a sharp knife and mark it down in sections – the skin will fall away.

Grapes
Skin grapes by plunging them into boiling water, then peel.

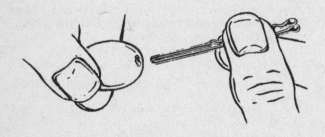

Fig. 6 Showing the rounded end of a hairgrip being inserted into the stalk end of a grape.

To de-pip grapes, push the rounded end of a hairgrip into the stalk end of the grape and prise the pips out.

Grater
Before grating oranges or lemons, dip the grater into

cold water: the peel will slide more easily off the grater.

Gravy
Don't throw leftover gravy away. Boil it up until it is thick, leave to cool then transfer into ice cube trays and freeze for use at a later date.

Grilling
Prevent grilled foods from sticking by brushing the grill over with oil before heating.

When grilling fish, cover the tail end with a piece of foil, thereby protecting it from drying out and breaking when served.

Guavas
Buy those which give slightly when pressed.

Hamburger
Speed up the cooking of a hamburger by piercing a hole in the centre. Once the hamburger is cooked it will close up.

Hazelnuts
To peel hazelnuts, toast them under the grill until the skins appear dry and cracked. Leave them to cool a little before popping into a polythene bag. Then rub against one another until the skins peel away.

Herbs
Dried herbs are best stored in dark glass jars placed somewhere cool. Light destroys both their flavour and colour.

Honey
If honey has gone hard, stand it in a bowl of hot water to return it to its normal consistency.

Ice Cream
When spooning ice cream straight from the freezer dip the spoon in warm water first.

Never re-freeze ice cream. Exposure to the air causes ice crystals to form which in turn spoils the texture of the ice cream and also its taste.

Be creative and add some crushed ginger nut biscuits, chocolate pieces, coconut or a spoon of tangy marmalade to ice cream.

Ice Cubes – see also *Fruit Juices,* page 87; *Lemon,* page 92.
Trays from boxes of chocolates make decorative ice cube containers.

Boiled water which has been left to cool is better to use for making ice cubes. The cubes will freeze quicker and the ice will be crystal clear.

Jam
To prevent mould forming on jam, store it in an airy, dry, but cool place.

To test whether home made jam is ready to set, put a spoonful onto a saucer then into the fridge. After 60 seconds draw a finger through the jam and if it is ready the surface will wrinkle up.

Jelly
To unmould a jelly, stand the mould in a bowl of warm water for a few seconds.

Add ice cubes for a quicker setting jelly. Melt the jelly using half the amount of boiling water, bring to the full amount by adding ice cubes.

Liven up a jelly by popping some fruit inside, or, when making individual ones, put a jelly baby on the bottom of each mould.

Ketchup
If ketchup won't flow out from the bottle, push a straw

Fig. 7 Showing a ketchup bottle with a straw being pushed in.

into the middle and out again to allow the air to get flowing.

Kidneys
To improve the flavour of ox and veal kidney, soak them in salted water or milk for a few hours.

Kippers – see also *Smells* (Domestic Tips, page 54).

An easy way to cook kippers. Stand them in a jug and pour boiling water over, leave for 5 – 10 minutes, depending on their size, drain and serve with pats of butter.

When grilling kippers keep them moist by putting a tablespoon of water under the grill. Otherwise they will tend to dry out.

Kiwi Fruit

If you find kiwi fruit rather messy to eat, cut off the top end and eat with a teaspoon, rather like a boiled egg.

Kiwi fruits are ripe to eat if, when pressed, they give a little.

Lamb – see *Glaze,* page 87.

Lasagne

Because lasagne often sticks together whilst cooking, put the sheets in separately, allowing the water to come back to the boil after each addition.

Leeks

Wrap leeks well when storing, otherwise their smell will pervade everything else.

Small slim leeks taste better than larger ones.

Lemon

To extract more juice from a lemon, pop it in the microwave on a low setting for one minute. If you haven't got a microwave, roll the lemon in between your hands before squeezing it.

Buy lemons when they are cheap and freeze the juice into ice cubes. Store the cubes in a polythene bag.

Lettuce
When drying a large amount of lettuce pop it into a clean pillowcase and put it into the spin dryer for 30 seconds or so.

Lettuce is less likely to wilt if it is broken instead of cut up.

Liver
Fresh liver will be more tender if dipped in milk for a few minutes before cooking.

Liver will be easier to hold if it is first rolled in flour.

Lobster
Enhance the flavour of lobster by sprinkling it lightly with salt, a touch of black pepper and lemon juice whilst defrosting.

Lychees
Pinch the skin of a fresh lychee until it cracks and it will be easier to peel.

Mangoes
When mangoes are ripe they should yield to gentle pressure and will store very well in a refrigerator.

Margarine
It is advisable to use hard margarine when the recipe denotes the fat has to be rubbed or rolled. Because soft margarine contains a higher percentage of oils and it creams quickly, it is better used for all-in-one cake recipes.

Marmalade
Before potting marmalade, cool for several minutes, then give it a good stir, to ensure the fruit remains suspended.

Marzipan
Roll marzipan out inside a polythene bag; it's less messy than rolling it out on the worktop. When required, snip the top of the bag and lift out.

Melons
Use an ice cream scoop to de-seed melons.

Judge the ripeness of a melon by its smell, which should be sweet and distinctive.

Microwaving
Clingfilm makes a good transparent lid, provided it doesn't actually touch the food. For dishes which emit a lot of fat but do not necessarily require a lid to retain moisture, absorbent paper is useful.

If food needs to be stirred whilst in the microwave, leave a corner folded back.

Because cake or steamed pudding mixture rises a lot during baking use a large container and make sure it's only half full of the mixture.

Milk
Although dried skimmed milk does not always give the same results it can be used in an emergency in a recipe to replace fresh milk.

Milk that is being boiled won't stick if the pan is rinsed with cold water before using.

Mince
For spicier tasting mince, add ½ teaspoonful of mild curry powder to it when cooking.

Mincemeat
Grated lemon rind gives a tangy flavour to mince pie pastry.

If mincemeat appears dry, put a tablespoon of grated apple in.

Mint
Chopping fresh mint can be made easier if the leaves are sprinkled with sugar.

Make lots of fresh mint sauce and freeze in ice cube trays to use during the winter.

Muffins
Wholemeal halved muffins are ideal for mini pizza bases.

Mushrooms
When frying mushrooms, pop a teaspoonful of lemon juice in with the butter – it will keep the mushrooms white and firm.

Don't peel mushrooms, simply wipe them over with a damp cloth.

Mustard
To prevent mustard drying out, add a pinch of salt.

Nectarines
Nectarines should be firm but not too hard.

To skin a nectarine pop it into a pan of boiling water for 60 seconds. Remove and peel.

Nuts – see also *Brazil Nuts,* page 81; *Walnuts,* page 103.
Store nuts in the freezer for a day before cracking them open. By doing so they are more likely to come out of their shells whole.

Packets of opened salted nuts, and fruit and nut mix, should be stored in a secure plastic container and kept in a cool place, preferably the fridge.

To chop nuts, put them into a polythene bag then crush with a rolling pin.

It is best to keep nuts in a dark, dry, cool atmosphere. Warmth and dampness impair their natural fat, and can make them shrivel, even in their shells.

Oil
Used cooking oil will last longer if it is strained and stored away from direct sunlight.

Olive Oil
Olive Oil will last longer if a pinch of sugar is added to the bottle and it is stored in the fridge.

Omelettes
After making an omelette don't wash the pan, simply wipe around it with a damp cloth.

For lighter omelettes add a dash of soda water to the eggs.

Onions – see also *Smells* (Domestic Tips, page 54).
No more crying when cutting onions if they are peeled under a running tap.

To store half an onion, rub the cut side with butter and lay it on a saucer; it will keep fresh longer and smell less.

To fry chopped onions without burning, cover them with water and add a little butter. Boil until the water has evaporated, then reduce the heat and simmer until the onions are a golden brown colour.

Onions, Spring
To peel spring onions, plunge into boiling water for 60 seconds: the skin will fall away.

Oranges – see also *Grater,* page 88; *Ice Cubes,* page 90.
   Frozen oranges are easier to grate, so pop them into the freezer for an hour or two before required.

   Oranges will peel more speedily if put into a microwave on a low setting for 60 seconds. You will also be able to extract more juice.

Packed Lunches/Picnics – see *Quiches,* page 99; *Rolls,* page 100.

Pancakes
   Pile ready-to-serve pancakes on a plate over a pan of boiling water and cover with a tea towel in order to retain their heat.

Papayas
   This fruit is ready to eat when the skin has turned from green to yellow and gives slightly when pressed.

Parsley
   To crush parsley put it in a polythene bag and freeze it. Afterwards it can be easily crushed in the bag.

Pasta
   Stop pasta bubbling over or sticking together when cooking by putting a knob of butter or a tablespoon of oil into the water.

   To reheat cold pasta pour boiling water over.

Pastry – see also *Pies,* page 99; *Plums,* page 99.
   Wrap and chill pastry 10 – 15 minutes before rolling out. This helps it relax and makes rolling out easier.

   When baking blind, line the pastry with tissue paper instead of greaseproof. Although the latter is more commonly used when baking blind, tissue paper causes far less damage to the pastry case because it crumples more easily.

Use chilled water and a squeeze of lemon juice when mixing puff and flaky pastry.

For a sweet, crispy crust to fruit tarts, paint the pastry around the edges with beaten egg white. Sprinkle over with caster sugar.

Peaches
To skin a peach, pop it into a pan of boiling water for 60 seconds. Remove and peel.

Peel firm skinned peaches with a potato peeler.

To ripen peaches put them into a box and cover with several layers of newspaper.

Pears
Pears ripen as a normal process when they are put in room temperature.

Peas
Frozen peas taste delicious if a teaspoonful of mint jelly is added to the pan whilst boiling.

Boil fresh peas in their pods; when they are ready the pods will rise to the top.

Peppers
Peppers should have shiny skins and feel firm to the touch. Softness indicates they are past their best.

Skin peppers by blistering their outsides quickly under a hot grill. Plunge them into cold water and the skin will rub off.

Pies
Keep pastry moist when reheating pies by placing a small dish of water in the oven.

Pineapple
Use a pastry cutter to stamp out the core of a pineapple.

Pizzas – see *Muffins, page 95*.

Plums
Cherry or plum stones boiled, then rinsed and dried, make a perfect filling when baking blind.

Poppadoms
For less fattening poppadoms, don't fry them, instead place them in a microwave for 30 seconds.

Porridge
Make the porridge pan easier to clean by melting in it a knob of butter before preparing the porridge; or fill the pan with cold water immediately the porridge is served.

Potatoes
Before scraping new potatoes, place them in a bowl of warm water for several minutes; the skins will then slide off.

Potatoes will cook quicker if cut lengthways.

If you sprinkle roast potatoes with a little flour halfway through baking time they will turn out crisper.

For tastier and whiter potatoes, add a little nutmeg when they are mashed.

Quiches
Take a warm quiche on a picnic – when it has been cooked, wrap it in foil and then in several layers of newspaper. This will keep it warm for several hours.

Quiches can be taken straight from the freezer and reheated in a hot oven.

Raisins
To revive dried up looking raisins, place them in a bowl and sprinkle a little water over them. Pop into the fridge for half an hour.

Raspberries
Leave them with their stalks on, unwashed and spread out in the fridge to enable air to circulate. Once sugar is put over them, they soften.

Redcurrants
As for blackcurrants, page 80.

Rhubarb
When buying rhubarb remember, thinner stems are more tender. Store them in a cool dry place.

Rice
When cooking rice, add a few drops of lemon to the water to keep it white.

Rolls
When freezing rolls for packed lunches, slit them first. When you remove them from the freezer there is no need to defrost them, simply butter and fill.

Salami
Meats such as salami may 'go off' after cutting, so cover in foil and store in the fridge. Eat within a few days.

Salt
Add several grains of rice to your salt cellar to keep it free flowing.

Sardines
Turn over cans of sardines from time to time, allowing

the oil to run through. They mature and improve the longer they are kept (within reason!).

Sauces

To keep a sauce hot and free from skin, pour it into a "thermos" flask.

Sausages

Roll sausages in flour before frying to improve their browning.

Shellfish

If shellfish is not very fresh it could cause food poisoning. Live shellfish ought to be stored in ice or preferably sea water; however, lobster and crab will keep well if wrapped in damp newspaper in a fridge for 24 hours because newspaper retains moisture for longer and so, in turn, will keep the fish fresher for longer. Most shellfish will store up to 1 month in a freezer.

Soups

When making soup to freeze, after it has cooled pour it into a polythene bag and then place inside the plastic container. Once frozen, the polythene bag is removed from the container and slipped into the freezer making a more compact shape for storing.

Spinach

Spinach shrinks a lot when it is cooking so always buy more than you think you require.

Stock Cubes

The fridge is the best place to store stock cubes; when required they will crumble much better.

Strawberries

The juice of an orange poured over a bowl of strawberries enhances their flavour.

When buying strawberries choose those with their hulls on.

Sugar
Icing sugar is best left in its original wrapper. Once opened, sieve before using, and seal the residue well.

Sweetcorn
Sweetcorn is at its freshest when pale in colour.

Syrups
When spooning out syrup or treacle, warm the spoon first and the mixture will slide off easily.

Tomatoes
Tomatoes which are deep red in colour and soft to the touch are over ripe and better fried or grilled.

To skin tomatoes without their turning soft, dip into fast boiling water for 8–10 seconds then plunge into cold water.

Store tomatoes in the fridge. When required, take them out at least half an hour beforehand, to get them accustomed to room temperature.

Trifles
Stale sponge cakes are perfect for trifles.

Turkey
When cooking, cover the breast with foil to prevent it burning. Twenty minutes before it is cooked, remove the foil, thereby allowing the skin to crisp and turn brown.

Because turkey is a dry bird, keep it moistened and rub it all over with softened butter or margarine before cooking.

Veal
Buy veal which is pink and moist.

Because veal lacks fat and dries out quickly it is best cooked in a roasting bag.

Vegetables
When blanching vegetables, put them into net bags made up from old net curtains. This makes the job of transferring them from hot water into cold far easier.

To retain their flavour, cook frozen vegetables in the least possible amount of rapidly boiling water, adding salt as required.

Cut vegetables in even slices, they will cook at exactly the same rate. Always undercook rather than overcook vegetables to retain texture.

Rub grease around the top of the saucepan rim to prevent vegetables boiling over.

Walnuts
Often walnuts can be cracked by simply crushing two together in your hand.

Watercress
When buying watercress look for fresh crisp bunches with dark green leaves, and check the middle to see that the leaves there are fresh looking too.

Watercress wilts quickly. If the leaves are dry and curling, lay them down in a bowl of cold water in a cool place for 2–3 hours.

Whipping Cream
Cream will whip up quicker if lemon juice is added.

Wine
Any leftover wine unsuitable for consumption can be

added to a casserole. Its acid content will help tenderize the meat.

Store wine in a corked bottle, laid on its side. Not only will the wine keep the cork moist and therefore easier to remove, but it prevents air from getting in, which could make the wine go mouldy or sour.

Yeast
Fresh yeast will remain at its best when stored in a container with a secure lid. It will last in a cool place for 4 days, or in the fridge for at least a week.

Yoghurt
Flavour home made yoghurt or commercially bought natural yoghurt with some coffee essence, drinking chocolate powder, diced fruit or mixed nuts.

Make an instant milkshake by whisking together half a small carton of fruit-flavoured yoghurt with a glass of ice cold milk.

Yorkshire Pudding
Instead of using all milk to make Yorkshire puddings use half a cup of milk and half a cup of water when making up the batter. All milk makes them heavy. Make sure the fat is piping hot before adding the batter.

6

PET HINTS

Abyssinian Guinea Pigs – see also *Guinea Pigs,* page 108.
Groom an Abyssinian Guinea Pig with a toothbrush.

Animal Hair
A damp piece of old towel rubbed along the carpet will
pick up any animal hair.

Animal Smells
It doesn't matter how well your animal is looked after,
there are occasions when it may become smelly, so ensure
that its bedding is washed frequently. Should your animal
have a persistent strong odour it may have a health
problem which requires medical attention, so take it along
to the vet.

Budgerigars
When buying a budgerigar make sure that you get one
from a breeder or a pet shop. A healthy bird will be:
lively, have a plump breast, glistening eyes, and appear
bright and cheerful.

If you want to try to train your budgie to talk, buy it
young and train from about 5–6 weeks old. Male budgies
are easier to train than female ones and seem able to
mimic a female voice, probably because it is generally less
harsh than a man's.

Fig. 8 A healthy bird will be lively, have plump breast, glistening eyes and appear bright and cheerful.

Normally line the cage with sandpaper to keep it hygienic and protect from infection, but if you run out of sandpaper then use some folded newspaper instead.

The average lifespan of a budgie is between 6–7 years, but some can live longer.

Canaries
Canaries live up to about 9 years.

They are generally quite happy to stay in their cage.

Roller canaries are the best type for singing.

Cats – see also *Kittens*, page 108.
Cats have an average lifespan of 14 years.

They are adaptable to most living accommodation, but are vulnerable to draughts, dampness and the cold.

If stray cats use your garden as a toilet, spread orange peel or pepper around the area – they hate it!

Dogs – see also *Dogs* under Safety Tips, page 140.

When choosing a dog as a pet, consider: size of your home; age of children (if any); whether you have a garden or a yard; whether the house will be empty during the day. Bitches are normally gentler and are therefore easier to look after as family pets. Mongrels make better pets than pedigrees who require much more attention, i.e. grooming if they are long-haired, etc., but they can sometimes be noisy.

If your dog shows any signs of tiredness, vomiting, diarrhoea, an insatiable thirst, constant urinating, its coat loses its shine and its eyes appear dull, then take him along to the vet for a check.

A ticking clock has been known to comfort and soothe a dog.

A bitch on heat can attract dogs from miles around so it is best to keep your dog indoors during this time.

Gerbils

Gerbils are happiest when in pairs but if you don't want them multiplying buy either two male or two female. They live quite contentedly together so long as they are from the same litter. Handle carefully, they are extremely energetic and can wriggle free quickly. Keep them away from damp draughty conditions.

Gerbils require a varied diet of rolled oats, wheat, sunflower seeds or one of the packaged foods available from pet shops. Supplement their diet occasionally with pieces of lettuce, sprouts, turnip, apple. Make sure there is always plenty of water provided.

They can live for up to 5 years.

Guinea Pigs – see also *Abyssinian Guinea Pigs,* page 105.
Use both hands when holding a guinea pig otherwise it could wriggle itself free, fall to the ground and escape.

They can live from 3–7 years.

Guinea pigs enjoy a varied diet of mixed cereals together with some green food such as cabbage and cauliflower leaves which helps aid their digestion. Alternatively, you can buy one of the packaged foods available from pet shops. Make sure there is plenty of water provided. A guinea pig having problems eating may require its teeth filing, so check this out with the vet.

Hamsters
These creatures make ideal pets, particularly the Golden Hamster. Choose alert healthy-looking hamsters which are 8–10 weeks old. Pick them up carefully as, like gerbils, they can wriggle themselves free, fall and be hurt.

They require feeding once a day and, although they will eat virtually anything, they do require a good diet consisting of mixed grains, fresh green and root vegetables. Only supply them with sufficient food for that day, i.e. about a tablespoonful of mixed grains and a piece of vegetable. If they get too much they will hold it in their pouches which isn't healthy for them.

They can live from 3–4 years.

Kittens – see also *Cats,* page 106.
Before buying a kitten ask at your local vet for names of reputable breeders. A kitten should not leave its mother before it is 8 weeks old. It should have been weaned for at least 2 weeks and had its required worming medicine.

Make sure you get a diet sheet so you know what it can and cannot eat. Choose alert, healthy-looking kittens with a glossy coat, sparkling eyes and a good set of teeth.

If you have a new kitten offer it a litter tray in which to carry out its toilet, positioned in a quiet spot, because cats don't like being watched at this time. As the kitten gets older, say around 3 months, and if you have a garden, take it out first thing in the morning, and then at intervals throughout the day. Until fully trained, keep kittens away from carpeted areas. The best way to pick up their excreta is with a wallpaper scraper.

At around 6–8 months male kittens are sexually mature. It is around this time they start to seek out a partner and do so by dispelling their potent smelling urine around the home. Because it is a noxious smell and often difficult to eradicate, it is advisable to get a tom cat neutered at 5–6 months old. Female kittens start their sexual encounters generally around 10 months. Vets may neuter a female cat at 6 months.

Kittens are very susceptible to feline enteritis and cat flu – it is wise to get them inoculated against both at 3 months.

Lizards

Lizards are growing in popularity as pets. They normally live up to 5 years. There are many varieties, so read up about them before buying one.

Generally they eat insects and spiders, but they also eat fruit and vegetables. They require multi-vitamins, powdered cuttlefish (from a pet shop) and drinking water.

As most lizards are wall-climbers make sure your vivarium has adequate room for this, as well as a secure lid.

Mice
Don't give them cheese to eat, it will make them smelly and fat. Feed pet mice raw fruit and vegetables. Food such as carrots and apples should be given daily but green vegetables should only be given in moderation, i.e. two or three times a week. A dog biscuit will also give mice something to gnaw at and keep their teeth sharp. They enjoy eating dandelion leaves, watercress and raw spinach.

Store their cage away from draughts.

Rabbits
Never lift a rabbit by the ears.

There are several varieties of rabbit which may require different care, so check this before buying one by asking pet shop staff or a breeder.

Rabbits enjoy eating green vegetables; root vegetables; oats; barley; they also enjoy toast mashed with milk as a treat.

Rats
Choose a rat which appears healthy with a shiny coat. Female rats are less smelly than male ones, but don't choose *Brown Rats* – they may carry disease. Rats can produce 6 litters a year. It is best to buy a rat when it is 5–6 weeks old, when they can be easily trained and tamed.

They enjoy ready mixed rat food but also require green foods (i.e. lettuce, chickweed) and fruit according to the season. Rats eat biscuits and bread mashed in milk. Don't feed them with cheese as it makes them smelly.

When picking up rats, grasp them around the middle and hold them securely.

Fig. 9 Hold a rat securely around the middle when picking it up.

A healthy rat may live for 3 years.

Tortoises
Because the import of tortoises is only legal under strict licences, many of the tortoises purchased in this country are British bred. Pet shops are not allowed to sell tortoises, so people must seek out reputable breeders (ask a local vet of any they know). Choose an adult tortoise with bright eyes, an undamaged shell and a clear mouth.

A tortoise's diet comprises assorted meat and vegetable and they may enjoy eating cat or dog food. They enjoy dandelions and also eat carrots and banana; a supply of fresh water is needed.

A tortoise will quite happily wander around in a garden so make sure there are no poisonous weeds lying around.

When the temperature drops in autumn and a tortoise

begins to slow down and eats less, it is ready for hibernation. Put it in a box with plenty of shredded paper, dry leaves or litter, secure the top and store in a garage or garden shed. There is no need to put any food or water in, as the animal has stored up enough food during the year. Check on it regularly.

7

CRIME PREVENTION HINTS

Answer Phone

If you have an answer phone, don't leave it on when going away on holiday as persistent callers will soon realise that the house is empty. Also, never leave a message saying that you are out; instead merely say that you are unable to answer the phone at the moment.

Anti-climb Paint

Anti-climb paint is ideal for applying to outside pipes and walls. It is a thick paint which dries on the outside thereby forming a thick skin, while underneath it still remains damp. When a burglar begins to climb the wall and touches the painted area his weight causes the skin to fracture resulting in a nasty mess!

Bicycles

Enquire at the local police station about security marking your bike, so that if it is stolen it will be easier for the police to identify.

Builders

Never allow a passing builder to undertake any work for you. Always go through a reputable firm. The Federation of Master Builders (see appendix) has a list of all creditable builders. Never part with any money until the job is complete, you are satisfied and have received a bill. If you pay cash, get a receipt at the time.

Burglar Alarms

Before investing in a burglar alarm, check that you have done as much as you can to prevent burglaries by having sufficient exterior lighting around your house; and that all doors and windows have strong, secure bolts and locks. If you would still feel safer with a burglar alarm system, there are many types widely available. Contact the National Supervisory Council for Intruder Alarms (see appendix); they will supply names and addresses of firms who offer advice on burglar alarm systems.

Burglar Deterrents

If you cannot afford a burglar alarm system, invest in the outer casing.

Take full advantage of the free advice offered by the local crime prevention officer in your area who will come and see you in your home.

Callers – see also *Door Chains*, page 116; *Door Viewers*, page 116.

Never allow a strange caller into your home without seeing some identification. All public service employees are issued with identity cards. If a stranger asks to use your telephone, refuse and don't allow him or her to enter your home. Offer to make the call instead.

Keep a piece of paper by the front door listing telephone numbers of the Gas/Electric/British Telecom. Should a caller say he/she has called to read your meter/check your telephone ask him for proof of identity. If still suspicious make a telephone call to the company before allowing him in. Make sure that the chain remains secure on the door at all times until you are confident they are *bona fide*.

Car

Ensure all locks work and remember to secure your car whenever you leave it unattended, for whatever length of time. Invest in an alarm and a steering wheel lock.

Car Park

When parking in a multi-storey car park, park as near as possible to the entrance where attendants are normally on duty.

Avoid using subways or alleys leading to car parks at night. Always have your keys ready so you aren't fumbling around in your handbag/pocket for them.

Car Thieves

Park in a well lit area with front wheels turned in towards the kerb – this makes it more difficult for a thief to steal.

Have the registration number etched on all windows.

Buy a wheel clamp especially if the car is stood outside overnight.

Caravan

To protect your caravan, if parked outside your home, jack it up and remove the wheels, or invest in a wheel clamp or a burglar alarm.

Dark

When out alone at night: never walk through a dark or dimly lit alleyway; always arrange a lift home or book a taxi from a reputable firm; always walk towards traffic, thus discouraging cars from crawling up behind; consider buying a personal alarm and carry it in your pocket; (ladies) always hold your handbag close to your body or if your handbag has a strap, wear it round your body with your coat over the top; if you feel intimidated or threatened by someone, scream and run in the opposite direction.

Door
If your front door is mainly glass, buy a blind or put up curtains to prevent people from seeing in.

Door Chains
When choosing a door chain, pick the strongest one possible. If in doubt, check with your local Crime Prevention Officer.

Door Viewers
Door viewers or peepholes are ideal, especially for the elderly. Make sure there is a porch light fitted outside so you can see who is calling.

Driving
Before going out in your car check: you have sufficient petrol; you have pre-planned your route trying to keep on the main roads as much as possible at night; you have some change and/or a phonecard should you need to telephone anyone; you have a torch at night.

Never: pick up strangers, however distressed they appear, instead find a telephone box and ring for help; leave your handbag in the front seat or anywhere visible.

Always: keep windows and doors locked if you have to stop for any reason; leave instructions where you are going, your route, expected time of arrival or return.

Elderly
The elderly are prime targets for burglars and tricksters. If you have an elderly relative living on his/her own, check with local Age Concern (look in Yellow Pages) who will be able to advise what, if any, financial assistance is available for security safeguards to their home.

The police are only too willing to visit pensioners' clubs, etc., and give advice on security measures – ask at your local police station.

Entry Phones
   An entry phone requires the caller to identify himself before gaining entry into the house. This is done by the householder pressing the button thereby releasing the door, however it is wise also to have a chain and a spyhole for added security.

Garage
   Always lock your garage, especially if it has an interconnecting door into the house.

Hedges
   A thorny hedge planted along the front fence of a house is a good deterrent for potential burglars, but it is important that visibility of the front of the house isn't totally obliterated, making it difficult for neighbours to spot an unwanted visitor.

Holidays
   Make sure you leave your house key in the hands of a reliable neighbour. Remember to leave him the address and telephone number (if any) of your holiday location.

   Ask him to check that any mailing literature or 'free' newspapers are pushed *right through* your letter-box.

   Advise the milkman and newsagent you are going away. If you will be away for any length of time inform the Post Office who will either hold onto your mail or re-direct it for a minimal charge.

   Don't leave blinds or curtains drawn when you go away, this will only attract attention to your empty house. Time switches, which can be pre-set to come on and switch off at various times of the day and night are widely available from DIY shops and are useful when away from home.

Check that all locks are secure, and put major valuables in the bank.

Don't lock inner doors or desks, a thief will only make more mess breaking into them.

Make sure your car is kept in view when breaking off a journey for refreshments if a roof rack (especially one securing cases) is on your car.

Home Security
If you arrive home to find signs of a break-in, go immediately to a neighbour's home and call the police.

Change front and back door locks when moving into a new home, previous owners may still have keys which fit.

Discourage "peeping toms"; close curtains after dark.

Store dustbins away from susceptible areas, i.e. roof extensions, garages, etc. A potential burglar could use a dustbin to gain entry into your house by standing on it to climb onto a wall or roof.

Invisible Beam Detectors
These are very useful to have outside the house. The idea is that if an intruder attempts to break in, his presence illuminates a security light which should scare him away.

Ladders
Never leave a ladder lying around where a thief could take it. If you have no garage or shed in which to store it, secure it against an outer wall using two strong padlocks and chains, one at the top and the other at the bottom end.

Locks

For extra safety it is advisable to have two locks on the front door, one quite high and the other at an equal distance from the bottom. The top one should have a deadlock mechanism whereby once locked it can only be opened with the key, whilst the bottom one should be a mortice deadlock, again only being able to be opened with the key. It is important to remember to lock them both whenever leaving the house.

Never discard an old lock – keep it in a bag with all related keys. On the next occasion you lose your key replace the lock with the original one.

Milk

Never leave milk standing on a neighbour's doorstep all day. If the neighbours have gone on holiday and have forgotten to inform the milkman, tell him yourself.

Neighbourhood Watch Scheme

If there is no scheme operating in your area, consider starting one up yourself. Contact the local police station for further advice.

Net Curtains

Net curtains prevent a thief from seeing if anyone is at home.

Receipts

Always retain receipts for expensive purchases to assist if there should be any insurance claims at a later date.

Telephone Calls

If you receive an indecent telephone call, don't talk however angry you may feel, simply replace the receiver. If you continue to receive such calls, contact British Telecom, who can intercept or perhaps trace the calls, and the police.

Windows

A rattling window indicates that it is insecure.

8

DIY HINTS

Air Bricks

Check that air bricks in the outside walls of your house are clean and free from any debris. Damaged air bricks should be replaced as soon as possible, otherwise unwanted rodents could get into your home.

Air Locks

To unblock an air lock in your taps, fix one end of a hose pipe to the hot tap and the other end to the cold tap.

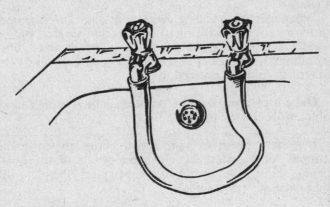

Fig. 10 Unblocking air locks in taps
Attach one end of hose pipe to the hot tap and the other end to the cold tap, and turn them both full on.

Turn both taps full on; pressure from the water should push the air bubble out.

Baths

Before filling in the area around the bath with any kind of sealer, clean it well using methylated spirit on a cloth, otherwise the filler won't stick properly.

Bicycle

Protect a bicycle from rust, particularly if it remains outdoors in all weather, by applying a thin layer of petroleum jelly over the framework. Stay clear of the brake cables, wheels and tyres.

Bucket

When decorating, pop a bin liner into the paste bucket. This will make the task of cleaning up afterwards so much easier, because all you need to do is throw the bin liner away.

Ceiling

When painting a ceiling use a paint pad. This is a piece of foam, covered with small bristles and secured onto a handle. It is less tiring to use, and helps cut down on those irritating paint splashes too. Also, wear an old hat or some other form of head protection.

Get a firmer grip on your paintbrush by sticking a piece of foam around the handle.

If using a brush to paint your ceiling, to stop paint dripping down your arm push the whole of the brush handle through the centre of a paper plate; the plate will then catch any paint spills.

To stop seams being visible when papering a ceiling, start at the window wall and hang the paper running parallel to the window. It is advisable to size the ceiling to stop the paper from sliding around.

When drilling into the ceiling, push the drill bit through an empty yoghurt pot first so that the dust will fall into the pot and not over you!

Chimney Breast

When wallpapering a chimney breast, hang the central part first then add the side sections afterwards.

Condensation

Condensation is caused when warm damp air meets a cool surface. To combat condensation: keep rooms warm, and have adequate ventilation; you may need to buy an extractor fan for the kitchen/bathroom; line kitchen ceilings with polystyrene tiles (however use flame-resistant types); make sure you have a good underlay under your carpet; consider double glazing (or put thick plastic sheeting up); line walls with polystyrene (which is available in rolls) before applying wallpaper over the top; make sure your fireplace has proper ventilation.

Cracks

To repair small cracks, mix the plaster to a thick paint consistency and use a brush.

Damp

There are many reasons for dampness outside the house, e.g. broken tiles, faulty flashings, fractured gutters and pipes. It is important to check all these regularly.

Doors

Seal any gaps between windows and doors with a strong mastic sealer. As the window frame shrinks and expands because of different weather conditions, so too will the sealer. Ordinary filler will just split.

Before painting a door, cover the handle with some aluminium foil to protect it against paint specks.

To prevent a door from sticking, run a candle along the closing edge.

Double Glazing
A cheap and effective method of double glazing draughty windows is to tape thick polythene sheets up against the windows.

Draught-Proofing
To draught proof around windows and doors use special plastic sticky-backed strips available from most DIY stores. They can be cut to fit any size door/window.

If you have draught coming through your letterbox, cover it with a piece of stiff felt.

Drilling – see *Ceiling,* page 122; *Tiles,* page 132.

Dry Rot
A rank smell often indicates the presence of dry rot which is generally located under the floor timber, in the rafters of the roof or the eaves. Stick a knife in the wood and if it slides in you may have a problem! If you discover dry rot in your house contact the professionals e.g. Rentokil.

Dust Sheets
Use old discarded bedspreads for dust sheets. Old pyjamas make ideal clothes when decorating.

Emulsion Paint
A roller is easier to use than a brush when painting with emulsion, as it won't leave any brush stroke marks.

In order for emulsion paint to stay on, areas must first be smoothed down and any flaking pieces sanded off.

Fences
There are many varieties of fencing to choose from.

Plastic fences, widely available in a number of heights and styles have the advantage over wooden type ones as they will not rot and require very little maintenance. Generally, wiping them over with a damp sponge will suffice.

Floorboards

Stop floorboards from squeaking by dusting talcum powder between the joins.

Small gaps between floorboards can be repaired by using papier-maché as a filling. Use an old knife to push the papier-maché into place. When dry, sand it down.

Furniture – see also *Garden Furniture,* below.

Heat marks can sometimes be removed from furniture by rubbing a small amount of turpentine into the mark.

A scratch mark can often be disguised by shading it with a wax crayon or shoe polish of a similar shade to the wood.

Fuse

To test whether the fuse in your appliance has blown, open the battery compartment of a torch and hold the fuse so that one end touches the end of the battery and the other end touches the terminal in the torch. Make sure that you are completing the circuit and then switch the torch on. If the bulb comes on, the fuse is okay.

Fuse Box

Keep a small card beside the fuse box indicating which lights and sockets are on which circuit.

Garden Furniture

When painting garden furniture outside, spread some sand or earth over the area. Any paint drips will fall on the earth or sand which then can be swept up and thrown away.

Paint wrought-iron (or any metal) garden furniture with enamel paint.

Gates
Repaint wrought-iron gates at least every couple of years. Scrub them down thoroughly with a wire brush and some emery paper to remove all loose bits, apply a coat of metal primer then an undercoat before applying two exterior coats of gloss or enamel paint.

Grouting
Use an old screwdriver to remove grouting.

Clean grouting around ceramic tiles with a toothbrush dipped in a watered down solution of bleach (make sure the toothbrush is *only* used for this purpose and that you wear rubber gloves).

Hammering – see also *Nails*, page 128.
Whilst hammering a nail into place hold it with a hairgrip. Reduce the risk of hitting your fingers when hammering in a nail, by pushing the nail through a piece of thin card. When the nail is firmly tacked in, tear the cardboard away.

Hands
Rubbing petroleum jelly onto hands before painting makes it easier to remove any paint from them afterwards.

Hinges
Handcream rubbed onto stiff hinges works just as effectively as lubricating oil.

Hooks
Make sure self adhesive wall hooks stay in position by smearing the sticky surface with nail varnish before fixing them up.

Kitchen

Any grease stains on wallpaper in the kitchen will show through new wallpaper. To stop this happening, you could apply some clear nail varnish over the stain to seal it and prevent it from showing through. But it is better to strip off the old paper altogether.

Use an oil-based silk-finish paint in your kitchen. It is more resilient than other paint to damp atmosphere.

Ladders

Make wooden ladders unslippery by painting each rung, but before they are dry, cover with a sprinkling of builders' sand, or stick strips of emery board on each rung.

Locks

Most stiff door locks can be eased if the lock and key are treated with graphite. To release a jammed lock, cover the key with some petroleum jelly and move it around in the lock.

Logs

Protect cut logs from dampness by covering with some waterproof sheeting. Don't pile them against a wall as they will stop the air circulating properly and can cause a damp patch.

Matting

If the edge of rush matting unravels stick it back into place using clear glue.

Moss

To remove moss from a pathway use one of the many fungicidal liquids. Alternatively, after removing as much as you are able to with a spade, wash the path down with a bucketful of tepid water to which an eggcup of bleach has been added.

Nails

When nailing into a plastered wall, secure a piece of sticky tape over the area where you intend working; this will stop the plaster from cracking and leave a nice clean hole when the job is complete.

Conceal an odd nail hole in woodwork by making up a thick paste of sawdust and glue and pressing it into the hole. After a while it will harden; it can then be sandpapered and painted.

Non-Drip Paint

Non-drip paints offer a more professional finish, especially for the novice decorator.

Oil

Remove oil on paths by warming up some builders' sand in the oven. When it is hot, sprinkle the sand liberally over the oil. Leave to stand for 5–10 minutes, then using a stiff brush sweep the sand off the oily patch so that it picks up as much as it is able to. The procedure may have to be repeated with fresh sand. Afterwards scrub the entire area with hot soapy water or a commercially bought cleaner.

Paint – see also *Emulsion Paint*, page 124; *Non-Drip Paint*, above; *Primers*, page 130.

Paintbrush

Remove all trace of paint from a paintbrush by dipping it into a jar of white spirit.

Before putting paintbrushes away, wash them out with fabric softener to keep the bristles soft.

When pausing from a painting job for a few minutes, cover the brush with some kitchen foil to keep the bristles soft.

Ensure a firm grip on your paintbrush by wrapping a

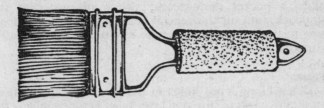

Fig. 11 A paintbrush with a length of foam around the handle for a firmer grip.

length of foam around the handle.

Painting – see also *Ceiling,* page 122; *Garden Furniture,* page 125; *Gates,* page 126; *Hands,* page 126; *Rollers,* page 131; *Skirting Board,* page 132.

If you have paint left over at the end of a job, put some into an old jar with a screw-top lid and keep for any odd scratches that may occur later.

Lemon slices placed around a newly painted room will banish any paint smells.

Lay a piece of wire across the top of the paint tin and use it to wipe the brush against and remove excess paint.

Prevent a skin forming on gloss paint by pouring a thin layer of white spirit on top of the paint before replacing the lid.

Pipes

To reduce the possibility of burst pipes during winter make sure they are well insulated. The cold water tank should be covered all over except for underneath, enabling rising heat to keep the chill off the tank and pipes.

If you do have a burst pipe:
place a bucket underneath; switch off water at the
stopcock; turn off the central heating system and immer-
sion heater; turn on all taps to empty the system; call a
plumber.

Plaster
When filling large holes in plaster, build up the filler
gradually, making sure one layer is set before applying the
next. Don't apply all the plaster at the same time or it
won't stay firm.

Plumb Line
A plumb line is important for establishing a straight
vertical line when putting up wallpaper or erecting a
fence. They are widely available from DIY stores.
Alternatively, make your own by tying a small weight, i.e.
a stone, onto a length of cord.

Primers
Primers help to smooth the way when applying undercoat to a surface. They also offer something for the paint
to hold onto and waterproof the area you intend working
on.

Putty
Before applying putty, dip the knife into some clean
water, so as to prevent the putty from sticking to the
knife.

When removing old putty, apply some paint stripper
and leave it to soak before prising out with an old
screwdriver.

Radiators
Patchy heat on radiators is generally caused by an air
lock so keep a special venting key on hand to release the

valve and let the air out; always place a bowl underneath the valve when you are doing so as some water may escape. The valve is normally positioned at the top of the radiator.

It is advisable to use oil-based paint as a topcoat when painting radiators. Vinyl emulsions can also be used but the radiators may require repainting more frequently.

To remove grease marks from radiators use white spirit.

For insulation, secure a sheet of aluminium foil behind any radiator which is on an outside wall; this will reflect a substantial amount of heat back into the room.

Rawl Plugs
If you have no rawl plugs, an old piece of plastic washing line cut to size will suffice.

Rollers
Clean a paint roller by rolling it over a newspaper to remove the excess paint. Remove the sleeve and wash thoroughly.

Rust– see also *Bicycle*, page 122.
Protect tools which cannot be painted from rust by covering them with a layer of grease, car wax or oil.

Repaint small scratches in paintwork before rust can develop. Emery paper is perfect for removing rust from metalwork.

Screwdriver
To prevent a screwdriver slipping, rub the blade with some chalk.

Screws
Loosen stubborn screws with a drop of vinegar.

Cover up screw holes in wood with a mixture of sawdust and adhesive. See *Nails* (page 128).

Rub screws with some petroleum jelly before securing into place: it will make them easier to unscrew later.

When tightening a loose screw, put some nail varnish under the head before screwing into place.

Shears
After wallpapering, put cutting shears into a jug of hot water for an hour to clean the paste off.

Sizing
Walls and ceilings should be sized before wallpapering or applying enamel/gloss paints. It removes any grease or oil and helps paper stick better.

Skirting Board
Before painting skirting boards, slip a piece of cardboard under the bottom to avoid picking up dust, or getting paint on the floor.

Tiles – see also *Grouting*, page 126.
Before laying or cutting plastic, cork or linoleum tiles, warm them slightly in the oven. They will be easier to cut and adapt to any unevenness in the floor.

Before cutting a polystyrene tile, heat the knife blade in boiling water.

When drilling into ceramic tiles, stick masking tape over the area you are drilling. This will stop the drill bit from skating around. Mark on the tape the required position of the hole, then drill the hole there.

Wall
Scrape algae or mould from an outside wall, then wash the area thoroughly using half water, half bleach. Leave to

dry and repeat the following day. (Always wear rubber gloves when using bleach.)

Wallpapering – see also *Bucket*, page 122; *Chimney Breast*, page 123; *Kitchen*, page 127; *Shears*, opposite; *Sizing*, opposite.

Washing-up liquid added to warm water makes wallpaper stripping far easier.

Make sure picture holes don't get lost when wallpapering. Push a matchstick into the hole and leave part of it sticking out. When new paper is brushed over, the stick will poke through.

To remove wallpaper bubbles, cut across them with a sharp knife (in line with any pattern) and carefully paste down the flaps.

Very few walls are straight: do not assume your wall is true. In order to ensure that you are working from a vertical edge use a plumbline to check it out. Regularly re-use the plumbline as you progress around the wall.

Use an old whisk to save time when mixing wallpaper paste.

Windows – see also *Doors*, page 123; *Double Glazing*, page 124; *Draught-Proofing*, page 124.

Remove paint splashes from windows as soon as possible with turpentine; if dry use a razor blade.

When painting window frames, stick damp strips of newspaper around the edges to prevent any paint specks from splashing on the windows. Afterwards it peels off.

Wood
To locate any unsanded pieces of wood, pull an old stocking over your hand and rub this lightly over the

wood.

A small dent on a piece of unpolished wood can be repaired if some wet brown paper is placed over the area and a hot iron gently put on top to encourage the wood to swell. Make sure the iron isn't left on too long! For polished or veneered wood go to a French polisher.

9

SAFETY HINTS

Baby's Bath
Always add plenty of cold water when running a bath
for baby and test the temperature of the bath water with
your elbow before putting baby in.

A small towel placed in the bottom of the bath will
prevent baby from sliding around.

Never run additional hot water into the bath once the
child is in.

Never leave young children alone in the bath for they
can drown in only a few centimetres of water.

Balloons
Never allow young children to blow up balloons, it is so
easy for them accidentally to inhale the balloon and
choke.

Bee Stings
Once a bee has stung its victim, its sting will continue
working until removed; do so with a pair of tweezers or
squeeze out with a clean finger nail. Afterwards, apply an
ice cube or cold damp cloth over the sting; this will cool
down the injury and reduce the itchiness and subsequent
swelling. If, after several days, there is any further
irritation inform your doctor.

Someone who has been stung in the mouth or throat needs plenty of iced water/ice cubes to suck and help decrease any swelling. Take him immediately to the casualty department of your nearest hospital.

If people have, in the past, suffered an allergic reaction to a bee or wasp sting, then the chances are they always will, so it is sensible always to carry some antihistamine tablets and proprietary sting sprays during the summer months. If however they have never had a reaction before, and suffer breathing difficulties, feel faint, sweaty and generally unwell, then don't hesitate: take them to the casualty department of the nearest hospital immediately.

Bees leave their stings in the wound but wasps do not. The most effective way to deal with a wasp sting is to apply antihistamine cream immediately to the area to reduce itching. If you have no cream of this kind, surgical spirit, calamine lotion or ice packs work just as well.

Bicycles
Never allow a young child to ride his/her bicycle on the road without having first passed a cycling proficiency test. Courses which are organised through Road Safety Officers are widely available throughout the country for youngsters. For further information contact the Royal Society for the Prevention of Accidents (see appendix), or the child's school.

Many unnecessary accidents happen to cyclists because they can't be seen, so have good lights, wear bright coloured clothing and buy some reflectors both for the bike and also to wear on the body. A crash helmet could make the difference between life and death. Make sure it carries a BS number, proving the bike has undergone rigorous tests.

Make sure that any bags carried on a bicycle are securely fixed to a luggage rack (usually situated behind the saddle). Don't hang them from handle bars – they could jam the spokes or, if heavy, unbalance the bike, and cause an accident.

Choosing the correct size of bike is important for children. To gauge this: with the child sitting on the bicycle and with the saddle (and handlebars) at their lowest point, the child's feet should touch the ground both sides.

When buying a secondhand bicycle check: spokes aren't bent or the frame twisted – could indicate it has been in an

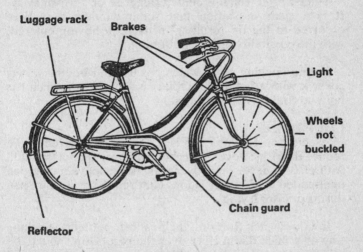

Fig. 12 A bicycle showing points of importance when choosing a secondhand model.

accident; the wheels aren't buckled even slightly; the brakes have a good gripping power and stop the wheels immediately; tyres aren't cracked – could indicate it hasn't been used for a while and the tubes inside could also be perished.

It is useful to get a good bicycle mechanic to check that a second-hand bicycle is roadworthy. Many bicycle retailers offer this service for a small fee.

Candles

If using a candle during a power cut, stick it in the bottom of a large basin with melted wax. Then pour some water into the basin. This should extinguish the flame if the candle falls over. Make sure you don't use a plastic basin – the melting wax could burn the plastic!

Cans

Tinned food which is dented ought to be thrown away. It is a clear indication that some damage may have occurred to the tin resulting in bacteria having entered, with the possibility of food poisoning.

Before opening a can which has been in boiling water, cover it with a tea towel. Otherwise the steam which has built up could give a nasty scald.

Chip Pan Fire

A chip pan catching fire is a common occurrence. To reduce the risks: never fill a chip pan more than a third full with oil and never let it overheat; never leave a chip pan unattended and never allow children near a chip pan during or after frying.

If it does catch fire: turn the heat off, put a lid, a baking tray or a thick damp cloth over the pan. Don't touch the pan for at least half an hour. Never use water to try to put the fire out. If the fire has taken hold, get everyone out, close the door and phone for the fire brigade.

Cigarettes

Fire resulting from cigarettes is very common. Reduce the risks of it happening: never smoke in bed; never leave your cigarette balancing on the side of an armchair in an ashtray – it could easily fall off and start a fire. Deep ashtrays are safer; they are generally heavier and there-fore less likely to be knocked over whilst containing a lighted cigarette. Never leave a cigarette burning in the ashtray, always stub it out. When emptying ashtrays put the ash into a tin can and pour water in before throwing away. Never put hot ash into a plastic bag/bucket.

Containers – see also *Cooking*, below.

Never leave containers of hot liquid, i.e. saucepans and coffee pots, etc., where youngsters can reach.

Never use drinks bottles to store poisonous liquids. Ensure that whatever bottles are utilised to keep noxious substances, they are well marked and out of harm's way, stored out of reach of children.

Cooker

Never position electrical sockets directly over a cooker. Don't situate a gas cooker alongside a window; a gust of wind could easily blow the pilot light out.

Cooking

Make sure pan handles are always facing inwards. If you have young children, make sure they keep well away from the cooker when it is hot, and invest in a cooker guard; this is a metal rail which fits around the outside top of the oven to prevent youngsters in particular from knocking the pans over. They are obtainable from many large department stores. See fig 13 overleaf.

Curtains

Don't hang curtains in a kitchen especially near to the oven. A blind is safer.

Decorations

Only buy Christmas decorations which are flame-resistant.

Fig. 13 Showing pan handles always facing inwards, complete with cooker guard around.

Dust Bags
When you empty the vacuum cleaner bags wrap the dust up in newspaper and pop it into a plastic bag before transferring into the dustbin. There is a lot of possible disease to be found in dust. Dust contains germs and can spread infection.

Dogs
Never leave a dog alone in a car with the windows closed. Always make sure one is open slightly and that the dog has some water to drink. Never leave a dog

unattended in a car during warm weather, even with the windows open.

Never let a dog eat from a human's plate.

Never allow a child to take anything out of a dog's mouth.

Doors
If you have all-glass doors in your home, make sure they are made of safety glass. Also, stick some transfers on them to ensure that people (especially children) see the doors and don't accidentally run into them.

Electric Blankets – see also *Electrical Overblankets* (Domestic Tips, page 39); *Electric Underblankets* (Domestic Tips, page 39).
Never use an overblanket as an underblanket or vice versa.

Electric Flexes
Never allow children or animals to play with electric flexes, in case they bite into them.

Electric flexes and leads from appliances should not be left trailing over the edge of the worktop. A child could easily pull the appliance over himself.

Electrical Appliances
If you have purchased a second-hand electrical appliance, make sure it is examined by a qualified electrician before using.

Check that electrical appliances are correctly wired to the plug, that the wires are gripped tight where they come out of the socket and that the plug contains the correct voltage fuse. See fig 14 overleaf.

When mending or repairing any electrical appliance,

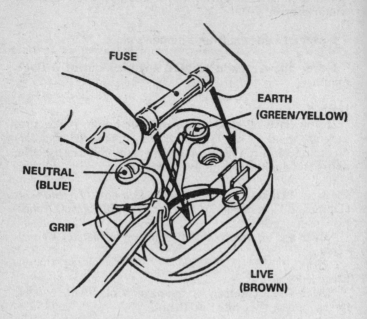

FUSE

EARTH
(GREEN/YELLOW)

NEUTRAL
(BLUE)

GRIP

LIVE
(BROWN)

Fig. 14 How to wire an electric plug
Wrap the wires round the terminal pillars (where present) in
a *clockwise* direction; the opposite may result in loose wires
when the screw is tightened.

ensure it is switched off and unplugged – people so often
forget this!

Electrical Sockets – see also *Kitchen Hazards,* page 145.
Electrical sockets are very tempting for youngsters.
Even with modern shuttered sockets it is advisable to fit
covers and remove temptation.

Always replace broken or cracked sockets and plugs.

Make sure you have sufficient electrical points so as not to overload those which you do have.

Electrical Wiring

Make sure the wiring in your home is perfectly safe and is in accordance with the safety regulations – if in doubt have a qualified electrician or the electricity board check it.

Fire – see also *Smoke Detectors,* page 147.

To reduce the possibility of a fire occurring in your home CHECK that: there is ample ventilation for boilers and open fires to burn safely; all doors are closed before going to bed at night in case a fire should start.

Never hang a mirror over a fire, as a piece of clothing could easily catch fire when the mirror is in use. Always keep young children well away from fires, especially when wearing night clothes which are flammable. It is best to buy children's clothes made from flame resistant fabric.

Fire Blanket

Invest in a fire blanket; alternatively a thick blanket would suffice.

Fire Extinguisher

Buy a domestic fire extinguisher – a 3 lb (1.4kg) one would be enough to cope with a small fire. Make sure you and your family know how to use it and that it is regularly checked and serviced.

Fireguard

If you have young children in the house it is important that you have a fireguard which should be firmly fixed to the wall on either side. This equally applies to any other form of open heating, i.e. paraffin heaters, electric fires.

Flammable Substances

Substances such as varnish, adhesives, paraffin, methylated spirits, etc., should be stored in air-tight containers and away from heat. Because they emit extremely flammable vapours, they could easily cause a fire if they come into contact with heat. Petrol should not be stored in the house at all but only in a proper container locked away in an outhouse.

Fridges and Freezers

Doors of freezers and fridges should always be kept closed. There have been many reported cases of young children, having been locked inside, suffocating. When disposing of a fridge or freezer, completely remove the door if possible, Otherwise, secure the door closed with some tape or wrap some string or twine around it.

Furniture

Make sure upholstered furniture is never placed close to a heater or open fire. Take care that no smouldering cigarettes or lighted matches are accidentally dropped onto it, since it could smoulder and catch fire.

When replacing or reupholstering furniture, make sure it is filled with fire-resistant foam and not ordinary foam which can emit dangerous and noxious fumes if it catches fire.

Garden Ponds

If you have an ornamental garden pond secure plastic garden wire, and/or a small fence around, high enough to deter inquisitive visitors who could so easily fall in and possibly drown. And make sure young children are never allowed near it unaccompanied.

Gas

If you smell gas extinguish any naked flames or cigarettes.

Don't use switches or the doorbell; they could ignite a spark.

Open doors and windows. Keep them open until all trace of the smell has gone.

Check that a gas tap hasn't accidentally been left on. Check that the pilot light on the gas oven hasn't blown out.

If there is still a strong smell: turn the gas off at the meter. Telephone British Gas immediately.

If the smell of gas is very strong, or if you are unable to turn the gas tap off, don't hesitate, get everyone out of the house and telephone British Gas and the police.

Gas Appliances
Whenever purchasing a second-hand gas appliance have it inspected by a qualified engineer before using.

In order for gas fires and heaters to burn safely there must always be adequate ventilation in the room.

When returning from holiday remember to turn your gas mains supply back on, and relight any pilot lights.

Home Hazards
Many household and shoe cleaning products discharge noxious fumes, so it is important that before using, all windows in the room are opened.

Always make sure that sharp items such as broken glass or razor blades, etc., are safely wrapped in newspaper before being put into the dustbin. If disposing of a large amount, then it is advisable to inform the dustmen.

Kitchen Hazards – see also *Containers,* page 139; *Cooker,* page 139; *Cooking,* page 139; *Curtains,* page 139; *Steam,* page 147.
Never store chemicals and cleaners under the sink; it is safer to store them in a locked cupboard or on a top shelf.

When buying a washing machine/tumble dryer ensure the door can be locked when not in use and that no little fingers can manoeuvre it open. It is amazing the number of times toys, pets and even children have been found hiding inside such machines.

Secure sharp-pointed kitchen instruments into old corks before storing in a drawer – in that way you won't hurt your fingers when searching for them.

Ensure that all new electrical sockets are placed at least 23cm (10″) above your work surface, well away from water, and never directly over a cooker.

When handling anything hot, don't use a damp or wet cloth, as water acts as a conductor of heat and can cause a nasty scald.

Meat
Cooked meat should always be stored separately from raw meat. If both are kept in the fridge, ensure they are well wrapped and kept well apart but on the same shelf (if on different shelves the juice from one may drip onto the other). After cutting raw meat on a board, scrub the board thoroughly.

Medicines
Always keep medicines out of the reach of young children.

If, for some reason, you don't complete the prescribed medication, flush any remaining tablets/medicines down the lavatory and throw the bottle away.

Microwave
When removing any covering from microwave cooking always start on the opposite side and pull the lid back towards you, thereby releasing the steam in such a way as not to cause a nasty scald.

Oil Heaters
  Oil and paraffin heaters should not be left in children's bedrooms; the heaters should not be left unattended; you should never carry a paraffin heater while it is alight as it could easily set fire to your clothing and furthermore, they should never be covered.

Power Cuts – see *Candles*, page 138.

Shock
  If a person is suffering from shock after an accident keep him warm with a blanket. Give him plenty of reassurance and call for an ambulance.

Slippery Footware
  Roughen the soles of slippery footware with sandpaper to avoid accidents.

Smoke Detectors
  Most deaths in fires are actually due to asphyxiation from smoke inhalation. Fit smoke detectors in your home and make sure they are checked regularly.

Steam
  When pouring hot water from a pan into the sink, partially fill the sink with cold water to prevent steam from rising and causing a scald.

Tumble Dryer – see *Kitchen Hazards*, page 145.

Washing Machine – see *Kitchen Hazards*, page 145.

Wasp Stings – see *Bee Stings*, page 135.

Waxing Floors
  Apply wax thinly and evenly over a floor; if too thick or applied unevenly it could cause accidents. Uncarpeted stairs should never be waxed.

Windows
   A piece of polythene sheeting makes a temporary repair for a broken window.

10

INDOOR PLANT HINTS

African Violets

When buying an African Violet choose one with sturdy healthy-looking leaves. They don't particularly like cool temperatures but love the atmosphere of bathrooms and kitchens.

Anthurium

These plants thrive in moist, warm conditions. When buying one, check it has a fair number of clean unmarked leaves.

Aspidistra

A popular indoor plant which requires very little attention. Buy one with plenty of fine strong stems.

Azalea

The Azalea makes an attractive indoor plant and is one of the few which bloom during the winter months. Choose one which has an abundance of buds and flowers. They enjoy a light location, but out of direct sunlight. Ensure they are never allowed to dry out, always using rain water.

Begonias

There are several kinds of begonia plants to choose from, either foliage or flowering ones. Whichever you choose, make sure that the plant is clear of pests and its leaves are unmarked by mildew.

Bougainvillaea

The Bougainvillaea is a sturdy plant and can be trained to grow around a constructed framework provided that it receives adequate sunlight. When buying, choose one in flower.

Busy Lizzie

Provided that you are ruthless about pruning, the Busy Lizzie will always be a profusion of colour. When buying, choose one that has plenty of buds and some flowers. They thrive in a light position.

Campanula

Perfect plants for growing from hanging baskets. They thrive in a light, airy position. Choose young plants with lots of buds and some flowers.

Chrysanthemums

Chrysanthemums enjoy a light, but not direct, sunny position and when in bloom the soil must be kept moist. Once blooms have died off they can be planted out in the garden.

Cineraria

They enjoy an airy, cool atmosphere, but not direct sunlight. Choose a plant which has an abundance of healthy-looking foliage and take care not to over-water otherwise it will cause the roots to decay and endanger the health of the plant.

Citrus Mitris

A very popular houseplant, the Citrus Mitris enjoys a sunny position, and doesn't like draughts. The soil must never dry out completely; however, over-watering may cause the leaves to change colour, so moderation is required. When buying choose one with shiny, healthy-looking leaves.

Cyclamen
A difficult but attractive plant to grow. They enjoy a light position, away from direct sunlight or any form of heating. Choose one with straight, healthy-looking stems and flowers.

Devil's Ivy
Devil's Ivy, with its pretty colour-edged leaves, prefers a warm, airy position away from draughts and direct sunlight. Water frequently with warm water.

Drainage
A coffee filter placed at the bottom of a plant pot helps drainage and prevents any soil leaking out.

Dried Floral Arrangement
Never throw bits of dried floral arrangement into the bin. All little flower heads, etc., should be saved for use in a future arrangement.

Easter Cactus
This very attractive cactus, which blooms in spring, enjoys an airy position out of direct sunlight. Water when the soil feels dry and don't feed when the flowers are in bloom.

Ferns
These make very popular houseplants and generally enjoy a shady location away from draughts and any heating systems. Watering should be done frequently; spraying on the foliage is preferable.

Ficus
There are many types of ficus plants, all of which require different amounts of light and positioning. None likes to be given too much water; weekly watering in winter and twice a week during the summer is generally enough. Never buy those with missing or marked leaves – they are a sure sign of old age.

Fuchsia
Fuchsias thrive in a humid yet airy atmosphere and need lots of water.

Geraniums
When buying choose a large, bushy plant. To encourage healthy growth, position where there is plenty of daylight.

Gloxinia
These plants enjoy being placed in the lightest possible position, but away from direct sunlight. Water generously throughout the summer but only occasionally during the sleeping, autumn, period.

Hanging Baskets
Several ice cubes dropped into a hanging basket each day saves stretching up with a watering can. To reduce water dripping from a hanging basket, line with a sheet of polythene.

Hibiscus
Hibiscus make super indoor plants. They require a light position, away from draughts.

Houseplants
When buying houseplants, make sure they are well protected before taking them out of the shop into the cold air, as the change in temperature could easily damage them.

Hydrangea
These attractive plants require careful nurturing. When buying, choose strong healthy-looking plants; those with lots of flowers are generally a good buy. They require to be kept cool and constantly moist to thrive.

Ivy
An ivy plant enjoys a light, cool atmosphere. In order to make it grow nice and bushy, nip out the growing buds

as they appear.

Mineral Water

Give houseplants a treat; after boiling eggs let the water cool and use it to feed them – it's packed full of mineral goodness.

Mother in Law's Tongue

This easy-to-care-for plant thrives in rooms with central heating and although it grows slowly it will live for years. Enjoys a high temperature and direct sunlight.

Poinsettia

A popular plant around Christmas time. They prefer a cool atmosphere. Keep them out of direct sunlight and also out of draughts. Never over-water. Let the soil dry out between waterings.

Polka Dot

This attractive plant enjoys light, but not direct sunlight which may damage its delicate leaves. Water regularly with warm water and don't allow the soil to dry out. During the winter months reduce watering. To encourage bushy growth, pinch out the tip of the stem.

Primrose

Compact but sturdy, the primrose enjoys a cool, light position, out of direct sunlight. Water every day. After they have flowered they can be planted out in the garden.

Rose, Miniature

These sturdy little rose plants enjoy a light position when in bloom. Don't over-water, but keep roots moist. Remove the dead flowers regularly.

Rubber Plant

Position in natural light, out of direct sunlight, and keep out of draughts. During the summer keep the soil damp; take care not to over-water during winter when the plant is resting. Sponge leaves with warm water to keep dust at bay.

Spider Plant
A very popular hanging houseplant. It requires a position in good light, out of direct sunlight and draughts; it needs plenty of space to grow. Water regularly during the summer to keep the soil damp, but less frequently during the winter; just sufficient to stop the roots from drying out.

Swiss Cheese Plant
This delightful plant needs to be positioned in a good natural light, out of direct sunlight. If it is kept in the shade, however, this may account for its leaves remaining fairly small. Water when the soil feels dry, adding warm water until it filters through into the plant pot.

Umbrella Plant
An Umbrella Plant enjoys a light, cool position out of direct sunlight and away from draughts. Allow the soil to dry out completely between waterings.

Wandering Jew
These plants look delightful when draped from a hanging basket. They enjoy a natural light, away from direct sunlight. When the soil is dry, water (use warm) very gradually. Spray occasionally with warm water.

Weeping Fig
Another popular houseplant which enjoys natural light, away from draughts and shady conditions. To preserve their glossy shine, sponge the leaves with warm water.

Yuccas
This robust-looking plant enjoys a warm, sunny situation. Water sufficiently during the summer to keep the soil damp, but in winter only water sparingly, when the soil feels dry.

Zebra Plant

Never leave this plant in direct sunlight, or near draughts; it will be happy in a location where there is adequate light. Water should be tepid and the soil given a good soaking, but it requires a drying out period between each watering.

APPENDIX

The Federation of Master Builders, Gordon Fisher House, 33 John Street, London, WC1N 2BB.

The National Supervisory Council for Intruder Alarms, Queensgate House, 14 Cookham Road, Maidenhead, Berkshire, SL6 8AJ.

British Pest Control Association, Alembic House, 93 Albert Embankment, London, SE1 7TU.

Royal Society for the Prevention of Accidents, Cannon House, Priory, Queensway, Birmingham, B4 6BS.

INDEX